# REAGAN, TRILATERALISM AND THE NEOLIBERALS

## CONTAINMENT AND INTERVENTION IN THE 1980S

### BY HOLLY SKLAR

DESIGN: MICHAEL PROKOSCH

SOUTH END PRESS
PAMPHLET NO. 4

## LIST OF MAPS AND BOXES

THE PROBLEMS OF EMPIRE   3
ANDREW YOUNG ON THE EAST-WEST
COMPETITION FOR AFRICA   7
MILITARY BASES AROUND THE GLOBE   15
ON PROPAGANDA   36
SELECTED U.S. MILITARY AND
CIA INTERVENTIONS   40
LOVELY PIECES OF REAL ESTATE:
U.S. TERRITORIAL EXPANSION   41
THE INTERVENTION RACKET   42
CORPORATE CAMELOT: GUATEMALA   60

---

Copyright © 1986 by Holly Sklar
Library of Congress Cataloging in Publication Data

Sklar, Holly 1955-
   Reagan, trilateralism, and the neoliberals
   (South End Press pamphlet; no. 4)
   Bibliography: p.
   1. United States—Foreign relations—1981-  2. Reagan, Ronald. 3. Trilateral Commission. 4. United States—Foreign relations—Nicaragua. 5. Nicargua—Foreign relations—United States. I. Title.
E876.S52 1986    327.73    86-6763
ISBN 0-89608-213-X

Special thanks to all those people who heard many of these ideas in talks over the last few years and gave me valuable feedback. Thanks also to Ruthann Evanoff, Ros Everdell and G.H. for their assistance on the expanding "Who's Who" among policy makers which informs this publication.

# TABLE OF CONTENTS

## 1
### STANDING TALL ON THE BACKS OF OTHERS   1
PAX AMERICANA TO REALPOLITIK   2
TRILATERALISM   4
Crisis Of Democracy; Global Accommodation;
Unmanageable Contradictions

## 2
### THE "RELEVANT" POLICY SPECTRUM   12
ROLLBACK   14
Egostrategics
LIMITED CONTAINMENT   19
Need vs. Want; The Credibility Quagmire
LIBERAL CONTAINMENT   25
Accommodation in South Africa;
Accommodation in Central America
REAGAN DOCTRINE   31
Shultz vs. Weinberger?
Low-Intensity Conflict

## 3
### THE NICARAGUA EXAMPLE   35
THE RIGHT TO INTERVENE   38
FORGOTTEN GAMBITS   43
CONTRAVENTION   44
PRETEXTS   46
Threat to U.S. Security? Electoral Farce?
Rejecting Peace Efforts? Freedom Fighters?
KNOCKING DOWN THE WALLS   58

## 4
### BEYOND ARROGANCE AND PARANOIA   62
THE DEMOCRACY DOCTRINE: A TROJAN HORSE   63
PERPETUAL SIEGE   66
IT'S MOURNING AGAIN IN AMERICA   67
CHANGE DON'T COME EASY   69

**FOOTNOTES   71**

**SELECTED READINGS   75**

**RESOURCES   76**

**ABOUT THE AUTHOR**

# The New York Times

**LATE CITY EDIT**

VOL.CXXX... No. 44,835    NEW YORK, WEDNESDAY, JANUARY 21, 1981    25¢

# REAGAN TAKES OATH AS 40TH PRESIDENT; PROMISES AN 'ERA OF NATIONAL RENEWAL'

# MINUTES LATER, 52 U.S. HOSTAGES IN IRAN FLY TO FREEDOM AFTER 444-DAY ORDEAL

## 'ALIVE, WELL AND FREE'

### Captives Taken to Algiers and Then Germany — Final Pact Complex

**By BERNARD GWERTZMAN**
Special to The New York Times

WASHINGTON, Wednesday, Jan. 21 — The 52 Americans who were held hostage by Iran for 444 days were flown to freedom yesterday. Jimmy Carter, a few hours after giving up the Presidency, said that everyone "was alive, was well and free."

The flight ended the national ordeal that had frustrated Mr. Carter for most of his last 14 months in office, and it allowed Ronald Reagan to begin his term free of the burdens of the Iran crisis.

The Americans were escorted out of Iran by Algerian diplomats, aboard an Algerian airliner, underscoring Algeria's role in achieving the accord that allowed the hostages to return home.

**Transferred to U.S. Custody**

The Algerian plane, carrying the former hostages, stopped first in Athens to refuel. It then landed in Algiers, where custody of the 52 Americans was formally transferred by the Algerians to the representative of the United States, former Deputy Secretary of State Warren M. Christopher. He had negotiated much of the agreement freeing them.

They then boarded two United States Air Force hospital planes and flew to Frankfurt, West Germany early this morning. They will stay at an American military hospital in nearby Wiesbaden, where they will be visited by Mr. Carter, as President Reagan's representative, later today. They will stay in Wiesbaden for a week or less to "decompress," as an official described it.

The 52 Americans were freed as part of a complex agreement that was not completed until early yesterday morning, when the last snags holding up their release were removed by Mr. Carter and

*Continued on Page A3, Column 5*

## Teheran Captors Call Out Insults As the 52 Leave

**By JOHN KIFNER**
Special to The New York Times

TEHERAN, Iran, Jan. 20 — The 52 American hostages began to roll down the runway to freedom today minutes as President Reagan was finishing his inaugural address.

As the Algerian 727 lifted off from Mehrabad Airport, ending 444 days of captivity for the Americans, they could see, most of them probably for the last time, a full moon picking out the distant white peaks of the Elburz Mountains to the north. The time was 8:55 P.M., 12:25 P.M., New York time.

"God is great! Death to America!" cried the young Islamic militants who kept custody of the hostages to the last minute, hustling them to the stairs of the airplane.

**They Soon Are 'Former Hostages'**

The American diplomats, Marine guards and the other hostages stepped one at a time from a bus, whose windows were covered with checked curtains, into a clear cold night. As they touched the tarmac, two young militants, the hoods of their parkas up against the chill, took them just above the elbows and propelled them through the shouting crowd toward the Algerian plane with its red stylized bird emblazoned on the tail.

Looking dazed, some with long hair and beards that contrasted with the neat trims of their official days before the embassy takeover Nov. 4, 1979, they stumbled into the first-class section of the plane. Now they were what a bulletin on Pars, the state press agency, would describe later as "former hostages."

"They seem stunned, as if they cannot believe they are going free," Ahmad Azizi, the Government's director of hostage affairs, remarked to an Iranian state television crew covering the departure.

At 8:20, the doors were sealed, Pars reported, and the engines began to whine. A

*Continued on Page A8, Column 1*

**11:57 A.M.:** Ronald Reagan being sworn in as 40th President by Chief Justice Warren E. Burger. Nancy Reagan held the Bible and Senator Mark O. Hatfield witnessed the ceremony.

## FREEZE SET ON HIRING

### Californian Stresses to Restrict Government and Buoy Economy

**By STEVEN R. WEISMAN**
Special to The New York Times

WASHINGTON, Jan. 20 — Ronald Reagan of California, promising an "era of national renewal," became 40th President of the United States as 52 Americans held hostage in Iran were heading toward freedom.

The hostages, whose 14 months of captivity had been a central focus of the Presidential contest last year, were flown in two Boeing 727 jets at 12:25 P.M., Eastern standard time, the very moment that Mr. Reagan was concluding his solemn Inaugural Address at the United States Capitol.

The new President's speech, made no reference at all to the long-awaited release of the hostages, but emphasized his present crisis, government solution to true problems, power the problem." And in keeping statement, the President issue for a hiring "freeze" as his first act. [Page B6.]

Wearing a charcoal gray cutaway, striped trousers and dove gray necktie, Mr. Reagan took his oath of office at 11:57 A.M. in the first inaugural ceremony ever enacted on the west front of the United States Capitol. The site was chosen to stress the symbolism of Mr. Reagan's addressing his own West, the region that served as his three Presidential campaigns of 1976 and 1980.

**Oldest to Assume Presidency**

The ceremony today, filled with patriotic music, the firing of cannons, the pealing of bells, marked the transfer of the Presidency back to the Republicans after the four-year term of Jimmy Carter, a Democrat, as well as the installation of the remarkable career of a conservative former two-term Governor of California who started out as a radio announcer and motion picture star.

At the age of 69, Mr. Reagan became the oldest man to assume the Presidency, and in five months he will be the oldest man to serve in the office.

Mr. Carter, looking haggard and weary after spending two largely sleepless nights trying to resolve the hostage

*Continued on Page B8, Column 1*

---

### More News And Pictures: The Inauguration

- The inaugural address............
- Agenda for the nation............
- Carter departs..................
- President Reagan's day.........
- Bush and Mondale................
- The mood of Washington........
- Portrait of Nancy Reagan.......
- A look at Reagan's West........
- The pride of Dixon, Ill........
- Senate weighs Reagan team......

### The Hostages

- Outlook for U.S.-Iran ties.....
- How the pact was reached......
- Text of Reagan statement......
- Reaction: U.S. and abroad.....
- Medical plans for the 52.....
- Elation among the families....
- A look at each hostage........
- How it all happened...........
- Chronology of the crisis......
- Carter statement in Plains....
- Woman remains in Iran.........
- The financial negotiations....

*Summary and Index, Page*

---

Anita Schaefer, wife of a hostage, embraced Mr. Carter at airport.

## Anxious Families and Towns Erupt Into Long-Postponed Celebrations

**By JOSEPH B. TREASTER**

Saying his final farewells at Andrews Air Force Base yesterday, Jimmy Carter spotted Anita Schaefer, the wife of one of the hostages, and exuberantly embraced her.

"Tom is in the air," Mr. Carter said, speaking of her husband, Col. Thomas E. Schaefer of the Air Force, who was the senior military officer at the United States Embassy in Teheran.

"Really, truly, Mr. President," she whispered.

"Really, truly — at long last," he said, "Tom is safe. I'll be with him tomorrow morning in Germany."

"Oh, thank God, Mr. President."

Then they both cried. And they embraced again.

**The First Glimpse**

As the hostages arrived in Algiers, relatives strained close to television screens for the first glimpse of their loved ones out of captivity in more than 14 months.

"There's Billy," cried Letezia Gallegos, as her brother, Sgt. William Gallegos, of the Marines, stepped down the ramp. His mother, Theresa, broke into deep sobs.

News that the plane carrying the hostages had taken off from Teheran came to Penelope Laingen, the wife of L. Bruce Laingen, the embassy's chargé d'affaires, as she sat in a reserved seat at the inauguration of President Reagan. A military policeman shouted the word for everyone to hear.

Some had gotten the word from radio and television broadcasts, and still others, like Marjorie Moore, the wife of Bert C. Moore, the administrative consul, received phone calls from the State Department.

Most of the homes of the hostages' families, torn by doubt, fear and anger for so long, exploded with joy. They cried

*Continued on Page A5, Column 1*

**12:25 P.M.:** Sgt. Joseph Subic Jr. propelled by militants to waiting plane at airport in Teheran

## A Hopeful Prologue, a Pledge of Action

**By HEDRICK SMITH**
Special to The New York Times

WASHINGTON, Jan. 20 — For a President who has promised Americans a new beginning, an era of national renewal at home and restored strength and stature abroad, the release of the American hostages in Iran was exquisitely timed.

**News Analysis** — The extraordinary deadline diplomacy that put the 52 captured Americans into the air over Iran minutes after the hostilities thundered a new leader into office provided a graceful exit for Jimmy Carter, a hopeful prologue for Ronald Reagan and relief for a nation weary from 14 months of humiliation and seeming impotence.

Almost unavoidably the human drama in Iran overshadowed an Inaugural Address that was less an inspirational call to national greatness than a plain-spoken charter of Mr. Reagan's conservative creed, less a sermon than a rousing speech, less a rallying cry than a ringing denunciation of overgrown government and a practical pledge to get down to the business of trimming it at once.

For all the new President's vaunted reputation as one of the nation's most polished political orators, his Inaugural Address offered surprisingly few rhetorical flourishes beyond the gentle tribute to ordinary Americans that "those who say that we are in a time when there are no heroes, they just don't know where to look."

Although Mr. Reagan made no direct mention of the hostages, their release was on everyone's lips. Moments before Mr. Reagan took his oath of office, word that the hostages were about to be flown out of Iran swept through the crowd stretched out before the Capitol, and though that news was premature, it provided the perfect symbolic backdrop for

*Continued on Page B7, Column 1*

# STANDING TALL ON THE BACKS OF OTHERS

*Paint RR as the personification of all that is right with, or heroized by, America...where an attack on Reagan is tantamount to an attack on America's idealized image of itself—where a vote against Reagan is, in some subliminal sense, a vote against a mythic 'America.'*
[Emphasis original.]
Reagan Campaign Strategy Memo
June 1984

Ronald Reagan's campaign strategists succeeded in their effort to make Reagan the personification of a mythic, *Heroic America* for millions of Americans—Indiana Ron versus "Wimp" Mondale and the "Temple of Gloom." *Heroic America* is white, Christian, patriarchal and preordained as Number One.

*Heroic America* is a National Insecurity State—a dangerous blend of arrogance and paranoia. Reagan campaigned on the slogan, "America is Back—Standing Tall." America the Victim has been besieged by hostile forces at home and abroad: welfare cheats, reverse discriminators, unilateral disarmers, Japanese carmakers, Islamic fanatics, Marxist-Leninist communist totalitarian terrorists. They're all out to get US. The Russians and their proxies are lurking just outside our many windows of vulnerability. So from Grenada to Angola to Nicaragua, America is Standing Tall on the Backs of Others. Proud to be a bully and call it other things: rescue missions, freedom fighting, striking back against international terrorism.

Sometimes, though, the players forget the script and speak straight from the heart. In February 1984, Secretary of State George Shultz visited Grenada and said: "The terrain is more rugged than I imagined, but it is certainly a lovely piece of real estate."

"Free World" is just another term for real estate. American Century real estate. "Freedom fighters" are the landlord's goons.

The Vietnam War and the Iranian revolution shattered the confidence of American Century Inc. *Business Week* did a feature story on "The Decline of U.S. Power: The New Debate Over Guns and Butter," complete with a weeping Statue of Liberty on the cover. In the words of the Middle East chief of a major U.S. bank:

> It was easy in the pre-Vietnam days to look at an area of the map and say, 'that's ours' and feel pretty good about investing there. That's no longer the case, as Iran has made so terribly clear. American investment overseas is going to happen at a reduced rate until we can redefine our world.[1]

## Pax Americana to Realpolitik

U.S. policy planners carried out their most successful effort to "redefine our world" with the construction of a *Pax Americana* amid the World War II ruins of German, British and Japanese imperialism. The Council on Foreign Relation's War and Peace Studies provided the basic blueprint for political, military and economic hegemony.[2] The postwar international monetary system, known as the Bretton Woods System, revolved around the U.S. dollar and the "Free World" flourished in the strong embrace of Washington's global military supremacy.

Business approved. As the president of Business International put it, "this was one of the periods of freedom: freedom to invest, freedom to trade, freedom to have economic intercourse. Stability and freedom."[3]

Within the United States, the postwar order was legitimated by the ideology of Cold War liberalism and enforced with wholesale McCarthyite repression. Cold War liberalism promised *guns* and *butter*: a strong national security state to contain the "red menace" and a strong welfare state to ward off economic depression, co-opt organized labor and keep people dreaming the American Dream.

By the late sixties, however, Cold War liberalism was in crisis at home and abroad. In March 1968 the unofficial group of political, military and business leaders advising President Johnson—the "Wise Men"—acknowledged the crisis in Cold War liberalism with their realization, following the Tet Offensive, that there was no light at the end of the tunnel in Vietnam.* Faced with a request for over 200,000 additional troops, most of the Wise Men told Johnson to de-escalate and press for negotiations: with public opposition rising, the war could not be won at a politically acceptable cost.

---

* In the words of Roger Morris, a former aide to Dean Acheson, McGeorge Bundy and Henry Kissinger, the Wise Men were "the most senior members of the foreign policy establishment—the 100 or so officials and ex-officials, patrons and proteges, who had dominated American foreign policy for the last quarter-century."[4] The Wise Men included McGeorge Bundy, national security adviser to Presidents Kennedy and Johnson; George Ball, former undersecretary of state; Cyrus Vance, former deputy secretary of defense and later secretary of state; John J. McCloy, former assistant secretary of war [the more honest precursor to "defense"]; Dean Acheson, former secretary of state; Henry Cabot Lodge, former ambassador to the United Nations and to South Vietnam; General Maxwell Taylor, former chairman of the Joint Chiefs.

## The Problems of Empire

Historical parallels can be overdrawn. But in historical terms, **the U.S. emerged from World War II as an imperial power and has had to live with the problems of empire ever since.** For great powers "to survive—and perhaps even to flourish," in the words of former Secretary of State Dean Acheson, their leaders must understand the connections between the military, political, and economic aspects of power...

1956-1965: **When empires cannot produce a commodity vital to their survival within their borders, they become vulnerable to decline unless they secure their sources of supply by effective military or political means.** For the Roman Empire it was grain from the then-fertile fields of Egypt and North Africa. For the U.S., beginning with the mid-50s, it has been the relatively cheap oil from the Middle East...

Cuba was to show another of the recurring problems of maintaining the American "empire"—an **inability to contain and channel the process of radical economic and social change in the Third World**...

1965-1970: Having taken on too large a share of the costs of collective [Western] security, **the U.S. discovered in Vietnam another of the ancient problems of empire: the high cost in resources of defending its perimeters.** With the Gulf of Tonkin resolution in 1965, the Senate almost blindly followed President Lyndon B. Johnson in committing an unsuspecting U.S. public to a land war in Asia. The costs of this war for a society that was beginning to commit more and more resources to meeting the ambitious social goals began to produce the economic strains—inflation and a weakened dollar—that have haunted the U.S. for nearly 15 years.

1971-1979: **The failure to protect oil supplies that began with Suez, combined with the economic and political strains caused by Vietnam, produced a long series of reversals for the U.S. in the 1970s**...The decade began with the collapse of the Bretton Woods monetary agreement...[in 1971]. That year also produced the first U.S. trade deficit of the 20th century, which fed protectionist sentiments in the U.S., including a domestic political assault on U.S. multinational corporations...The most serious blow of the decade, though, was the loss of control over oil supplies represented by OPEC's successful power grab in 1973...(Emphasis added.)

"The Decline of U.S. Power: The New Debate Over Guns and Butter," **Business Week**, March 12, 1979, pp. 40-41.

Richard Nixon and Henry Kissinger took over from Lyndon Johnson and produced another redefinition of U.S. policy. They seized the long-neglected opportunity to exploit the Chinese-Soviet split, strategically and economically, and re-opened the door to the People's Republic of China. Detente replaced the Cold War as the guiding strategy for U.S.-Soviet relations. Foreign policy was rooted in *realpolitik*, a less ideological, more pragmatic calculus of strategic, economic and political interests. Under the Nixon Doctrine, the U.S. attempted to delegate some of its responsibility as "global policeman" to regional deputies: Vietnamization under Thieu, Iran as gendarme of the Persian Gulf under the Shah.

It was economic policy, not foreign policy, that was Nixon's undoing among the Establishment. Inter-capitalist rivalry had heightened in the sixties as the West European and Japanese economies recovered while the U.S. economy weakened under the weight of guns and butter. In 1971 the U.S. ran a then-unaccustomed trade deficit, paying more for imports than it earned from exports. Monetary stability was threatened by a by-product of worldwide military and economic endeavors—a growing buildup of dollars outside the U.S.

Rather than negotiate necessary reforms in the international economic system, Nixon attempted to reassert U.S. primacy with a series of protectionist measures remembered as the "Nixon shocks" (e.g. import restrictions on Japanese textiles). International bankers and corporate executives were outraged when Nixon suspended the convertability of dollars into gold, breaking the Bretton Woods agreements.

As the seventies unfolded, the *Pax Americana* was challenged further by national liberation struggles in the colonies and neocolonies, OPEC oil "commodity power," Third World calls for a New International Economic Order and a deepening "crisis of democracy" at home. It was time for a third redefinition of world order under the aegis of trilateralism.

## Trilateralism

In the wake of the Nixon shocks, a group of multinational corporate executives, bankers, academics and politicians from North America (the U.S. and Canada), Western Europe and Japan founded the Trilateral Commission.[5] David Rockefeller became the North American chairman and Zbigniew Brzezinski the executive director. The key to trilateralism would be the "collective management" of global "interdependence" by the trilateral powers. Trilateralism advanced under the Ford-Kissinger Administration with the first Western economic summit.

With the election of Commission member Jimmy Carter in 1976, trilateralism had an unprecedented chance to move from theory to practice. As former National Security Adviser Zbigniew Brzezinski notes in his autobiography, "all the key foreign policy decision makers of the Carter Administration had previously served in the Trilateral Commission."[6] These included, among others, Vice President Walter

Mondale, Secretary of State Cyrus Vance, Defense Secretary Harold Brown, Treasury Secretary W. Michael Blumenthal, Arms Control and Disarmament Agency Director Paul Warnke and United Nations Ambassador Andrew Young.

## Crisis of Democracy

Unfortunately for Carter, the president could no longer "govern the country with the cooperation of a relatively small number of Wall Street lawyers and bankers," as a Trilateral Commission report described an earlier era. In the U.S. section of that report, *The Crisis of Democracy*, Samuel Huntington (coordinator of national security on the National Security Council, 1977-78, and a "regular consultant" to the CIA during the 1960s)[7] laments the erosion of traditional forms of public and private authority and the widespread questioning of "the legitimacy of hierarchy, coercion, discipline, secrecy, and deception—all of which are, in some measure, inescapable attributes of the process of government."[8] The crisis of democracy was that too many people participated too much, or attempted to do so—Congress, the media, "value-oriented intellectuals" and, most importantly, the public:

> Previously passive or unorganized groups in the population, blacks, Indians, Chicanos, white ethnic groups, students, and women now embarked on concerted efforts to establish their claims to opportunities, positions, rewards, and privileges, which they had not considered themselves entitled to before.[9]

The "minorities" and "special interests," representing most of the population, were challenging the Establishment which ruled in the holy name of the National Interest. The *Crisis of Democracy* was unusually blunt about the distinction between egalitarian, participatory democracy and the anemic democracy beloved by the Establishment: "The effective operation of a democratic political system usually requires some measure of apathy and noninvolvement on the part of some [i.e. most] individuals and groups."[10] The greatest threat to democracy is democracy itself:

> The vulnerability of democratic government in the United States thus comes not primarily from external threats, though such threats are real, nor from internal subversion from the left or the right, although both possibilities could exist, but rather from the internal dynamics of democracy itself in a highly educated, mobilized, and participant society.[11]

Dan Wasserman

If peoples' expectations of government were getting out of hand and democracy was running amuck, it was time for apathy and the "politics of less" enforced through recession, austerity and a blame-the-victim campaign against the "special interests." As usual, Corporate America's counterattack would be cloaked in the mantle of the National Interest.

Jimmy Carter was the first neoliberal president. He made fiscal conservatism the bipartisan alternative to the Welfare State. *Business Week* asserted in 1979: "If the decline in U.S. power is to be arrested, the trend toward spending a smaller share of the federal budget on defense must be reversed, and economic policy must change in a way that encourages investment at the expense of consumption."[12] Trilateralist Federal Reserve Chairman Paul Volcker put it even more bluntly: "The standard [of living] of the average American has to decline."[13]

## Accommodation: Shaping the Forces of History

A minimum of social justice and reform will be necessary for stability in the long run.
  *Towards a Renovated International System,* Trilateral Commission, 1977

According to Brzezinski, the Carter Administration had ten basic foreign policy objectives:

1. To engage Western Europe, Japan, and the other advanced democracies in a closer political cooperation through the increasing institutionalization of consultative relationships, and thereby to promote wider macroeconomic coordination pointing toward a stable and open monetary system.

2. To weave a worldwide web of bilateral, political, and, where appropriate, economic relations with the new emerging regional "influentials," [e.g. Venezuela, Brazil, Nigeria, Saudi Arabia, Iran, India and Indonesia] thereby widening, in keeping with historical circumstances, our earlier reliance on the Atlantic community.

3. To develop more accommodating North-South relations, political as well as economic [e.g. Panama Canal Treaty], so as to develop greater economic stability and growth in the Third World, diminish hostility toward the U.S., lessen Soviet influence, and increase the stake those nations would have in good relations with the North and the West.

4. To push U.S.-Soviet strategic arms *limitation* talks into strategic arms *reduction* talks, using the foregoing as an entering wedge for a more stable U.S.-Soviet relationship. At the same time, we wanted to rebuff Soviet incursions both by supporting our friends and by ameliorating the sources of conflict which the Soviets exploit. We wanted to match Soviet ideological expansion by a more affirmative American posture on global human rights, while seeking consistently to make detente both more comprehensive and more reciprocal.

5. To normalize U.S.-Chinese relations because we saw that relationship as a central stabilizing element of our global policy and a keystone for peace.

6. To obtain a comprehensive Middle East settlement, without which the further radicalization of the Arab world and the reentry of the Soviet Union into the Middle East could not be avoided.

7. To set in motion a progressive and peaceful transformation of South Africa toward a biracial democracy while in the meantime forging elsewhere a coalition of moderate black African leaders in order to stem continental radicalization and

eliminate the Soviet-Cuban presence from the continent. We wanted to help achieve majority rule in Zimbabwe...

8. To restrict the level of global armaments, unilaterally and through international agreements...cooperate in international restraints on nuclear proliferation and sign a Comprehensive Test Ban Treaty...ratify the Threshold Test Ban Treaty [and] the Peaceful Nuclear Explosion Treaty.

9. To enhance global sensitivity to human rights...

10. To maintain a defense posture capable of deterring the Soviet Union, both on the strategic and the conventional level, from hostile acts and from political pressure.[14]

Speaking about change in the Third World, Brzezinski explained that the Carter Administration "is not trying to build dams against the forces of history but rather to channel these forces in a positive direction."[15] The "positive direction," of course, is the direction which serves the interest of Western capitalism. A fundamental premise of accommodation was the belief that the West could beat the Soviet Union at the "development game" of aid, trade and investment. Blind confrontation in defense of the status quo along the lines of a military chess game would only give the Soviets more opportunities for influence and risk a no-win superpower showdown.

## Andrew Young on the East-West Competition For Africa

The blunting of the Soviet political advantage in Africa...continued with the promulgation of the Anglo-American Plan for Zimbabwean independence and the Western initiative on Namibia in 1977, and then with the Lancaster House talks on Zimbabwe in 1979. This process must be viewed as an example of highly effective implementation of the Carter Administration's strategy of protecting American strategic interests through diplomatic means...

Just five years ago, the prospects for African-American relations were extremely bleak...The prospect of Soviet hegemony over the resource-rich southern African region represented a serious strategic threat to Western interests, and much of Africa saw armed struggle with Soviet weapons as the only course to the total decolonization of the continent...

Nothing has affected the East-West competition for African influence and resources as much as the African realization that the problems of hunger, disease, illiteracy and underdevelopment are equally as intractable as the problems of racism and colonialism...

Despite embarrassingly low levels of official development assistance by the West, the availability of Western private investment and a century-long commitment of Christian missionary education have given the West an almost complete domination over the Soviet bloc when it comes to African development.

Source: Andrew Young, "The United States and Africa: Victory for Diplomacy," **Foreign Affairs: America and the World 1980,** pp. 649 and 656.

Debt Diplomacy replaced Gunboat Diplomacy as the weapon of choice in enforcing neocolonialism (formal political independence with economic dependence). For example, following an unsuccessful CIA campaign to destabilize the Manley government, the Jamaican experiment in democratic socialism was derailed in large part through the International Monetary Fund's program of austerity and "stabilization," which undermined the economic and social progress upon which Manley's popularity was based.

In southern Africa, the strategy was to take the battle for majority rule off the battlefield and into the conference room. The U.S. and Britain worked together to arrange an independence settlement for Zimbabwe which, it was hoped, would preserve neocolonialism as it dismantled white-settler colonialism. In Namibia, a Contact Group made up of five Western powers—the U.S., Britain, Canada, West Germany and France—negotiated and renegotiated the basis for an independence settlement which included SWAPO (South West Africa People's Organization). This bold attempt at collective crisis management was derailed again and again by South Africa.

In Nicaragua, discussed extensively in chapter three, the counter-revolutionary strategy was to impose a "moderate" (i.e. pro-U.S. and conservative) government through a negotiated Somoza resignation or military intervention under the auspices of the Organization for American States. When that failed, trilateralists hoped to use economic aid to bolster the private sector and forestall Nicaraguan dependence upon the Soviet Union and Cuba by encouraging continued reliance on Western aid and trade.

The Carter Administration tried to learn from its too little, too late approach in Nicaragua and defuse the growing popular revolution in El Salvador by backing the reformist military coup of October 1979. Land reform (designed by Roy Prosterman, architect of the "Land to the Tiller" program in Vietnam) was seen as key to winning the population's "hearts and minds." But, as in Vietnam, land reform was always an appendage of counter-insurgency in the effort to reimpose "stability."

In February 1980, Salvadoran Archbishop Oscar Arnulfo Romero wrote to President Carter and pleaded that U.S. aid be withheld. He also called on Christian Democrats to resign from the repressive junta:

> Your presence is covering the repressive character of this government, especially abroad. You are an important political force. It is urgent that you question how best you can use that force in favor of the poor: as isolated and impotent members of a government controlled by the repressive military, or as one more force that incorporates itself into a broad project of popular government.[16]

On March 23, Archbishop Romero ended his sermon with these famous words directed to soldiers, national guardsmen and the police:

> We should like the government to take seriously the fact that reforms dyed by so much blood are worth nothing...In the name of God, in the name of our tormented people who have suffered so much...I beseech you, I beg you, I order you in the name of God, *stop the repression!*

Romero was gunned down the following day. Robert Armstrong and Janet Shenk write: "in the most bizarre rendition yet of the U.S. media's portrayal of the conflict, as a war between two extremes, the *Washington Post* reported on March 25: 'There was no immediate indication if leftist or rightist extremists killed the Archbishop. Both factions are waging a bloody war for control of the Central American nation.'" The day after the Archbishop's funeral, "non-lethal" military aid was approved for the junta, including cargo trucks, radar, riot control gear and night vision tracking equipment.[17]

As repression intensified and frustrated reformers left the successive *military*-civilian juntas to join the new opposition Democratic Revolutionary Front (FDR), the Washington propaganda refrain droned on to drown out the bullets of counterinsurgency: moderate centrist government battling the extremists of left and right. The refrain droned on even as the top five FDR leaders—including Enrique Alvarez, minister of agriculture until January 1980—were taken from the Jesuit high school where they were preparing a press conference and tortured, murdered and mutilated; even as four U.S. churchwomen were brutally raped and murdered; and even as two U.S. land reform advisors were shot down at the Sheraton International Hotel.

Three days before leaving office, Jimmy Carter broke the suspension of military aid which had been in place following the killing of the churchwomen and ordered an emergency airlift of military aid to El Salvador. His excuse? "Captured documents"—secret, of course—had revealed the guerrillas were receiving assistance from "Cuba and other Communist nations." Ronald Reagan would take the Carter pretext and run with it.

"Under Washington's new guidelines we've bagged our week's limit."

Bill Mauldin

In his memoirs, Carter has few words for Nicaragua and El Salvador. His final passage on the subject is self-serving, stopping short of his final actions as president:

> ...trouble was brewing in Central America. We were trying to maintain our ties with Nicaragua, to keep it from turning to Cuba and the Soviet Union, and at the same time to help the people of El Salvador...
>
> ...they are going through a blood bath down there...They don't have anybody in the jails. They're all dead. It's their accepted way of enforcing the so-called law.
>
> DIARY, DECEMBER 11, 1980

I was determined that the murderers of the nuns be brought to justice, that elections be scheduled, that some equitable system of justice be established and that promised land reforms be carried out. We had to convince the Salvadorans that brutal persecution of their own people was the major obstacle to their economic and political stability. Their top priority was to obtain more military weapons, but we held firm to our policy.[18] [Emphasis original.]

## Unmanageable Contradictions

By Carter's midterm, it was clear that trilateralism was in trouble. Instead of channeling the forces of history in a "positive" neocolonial direction, the U.S. was being swept up in the currents of contradictions. In 1980, Brzezinski expressed the central foreign policy contradiction, but he insisted it was merely two sides of the same coin. The Administration, he said, is trying "to do two things":

One: to make the United States historically relevant to a world of genuinely profound change; and secondly, to improve the United States' position in the geostrategic balance with the Soviet Union.[19]

For the U.S. to be genuinely relevant to Third World change, the U.S. would have to change its overriding goal of global domination. But trilateralism aimed for stability of Western dominance, not self-destruction. Brzezinski increasingly advocated militaristic geo-strategic policies at the expense of long-range accommodation; Vance continued to promote accommodation, with less success. Reflecting on the development of Carter's policy, Brzezinski writes: "I felt that the United States should use its power to improve the human condition, but I put stronger emphasis perhaps than Carter on the notion that strengthening American power was the necessary point of departure. Indeed, later on, when a choice between the two had to be made, between projecting U.S. power or enhancing human rights (as, for example, in Iran), I felt that power had to come first."[20]

The Carter Administration grew more confrontational as the "forces of history" appeared less manageable. Detente remained a two-way street: the Soviets were not embracing the icon of capitalism or tying their Third World policy to Washington's Good Housekeeping seal of approval. The post-Vietnam strategy of using "surrogate gendarmes" to police Western interests collapsed under the Iranian revolution. Rebellions and revolutions multiplied at too fast a rate for accommodation. The aim was to install pro-U.S. "moderates," such as Antonio Guzman in the Dominican Republic (success) or Shapur

## Standing Tall on the Backs of Others

Bakhtiar in Iran (failure). Washington could only attempt to cultivate good relations with so many radicals like Zimbabwe's Robert Mugabe (success) or Nicaragua's Sandinistas (aborted). Plentiful foreign aid, an essential element of accommodation, was not forthcoming from Congress. And, after the Camp David Accords, Israel and Egypt split the lion's share of foreign aid funds.

Having "lost" Iran, the Carter Administration was determined to prevent further change in the Persian Gulf. Carter cried "Soviet threat" and launched the Rapid Deployment Force (RDF) in June 1979—months before the November 4 takeover of the U.S. embassy in Tehran and the late December Soviet invasion of Afghanistan. Carter unleashed the "new patriotism" with draft registration and hostage drama jingoism. The January 1980 State of the Union address contained the so-called Carter Doctrine: "An attempt by any outside force to gain control of the Persian Gulf region will be regarded as an assault on the vital interests of the United States of America, and such an assault will be repelled by any means necessary, including military force."

Carter also fueled the proxy Cold War with Cuba. In October 1979—after "discovering" a contingent of Soviet troops in Cuba which had been there for 17 years with Washington's knowledge—Carter announced the establishment of a permanent Caribbean military task force. He also pledged increased economic assistance "to insure the ability of troubled peoples to resist social turmoil and possible communist domination."[21] Meanwhile, Carter's 1980 Presidential Directive (PD) 59 committed U.S. war planners to prepare for fighting a "prolonged, but limited" nuclear war.

Resurgent jingo-militarism had its price. The SALT II treaty was never ratified. A diplomatic settlement in Central America, following the Zimbabwe example, became politically improbable. The pillars of trilateralist foreign policy—accommodation and detente—appeared to be made of sand. And, most importantly, by helping shift the policy debate to the right, Carter put himself and trilateralism further on the defensive.

By the time of Ronald Reagan's inauguration, the trilateral accommodationist consensus had fractured. In a 1980 address to the Los Angeles World Affairs Council, David Rockefeller asserted: "We cannot count on an alliance of angels to defend the free world."[22]\*

Writing in the Fall of 1980, the president of the Carnegie Endowment for International Peace, Thomas Hughes, observed: "Quickly unlearning all the harsh lessons of the recent past, many are tempted again to mistake a defense build-up for a foreign policy." Meanwhile, the "Great Simplifiers" on the Right "are striking the chords of mythology, petulance, false pride, and nostalgia." "American and world politics," warned Hughes, "are on a collision course."[23]

---

\* On a January 1986 visit to Argentina, David Rockefeller was greeted by demonstrators protesting his past support for the military junta. According to the *New York Times* of January 15, 1986, Rockefeller's visit provoked the worst street violence since the start of the Alfonsin presidency.

# THE "RELEVANT" POLICY SPECTRUM

Few in the politically relevant spectrum these days would challenge the assertion that the Soviet Union is a menace. Yet there is still disagreement about the nature of the beast and how to tame it.

Dimitri Simes
*Foreign Policy*, 1981[1]

Polarization has left the center looking more like the Bermuda Triangle. Politicians who go there tend to disappear. The rightwing undertow, combined with the disintegrating waves on the left, leaves very little in between except bubbles.

Thomas Hughes,
*Foreign Policy*, 1985[2]

Alexis Duran Llopiz

If the "politically relevant spectrum" for the Carter period ran from Andrew Young on the left, to Cyrus Vance in the center, Zbigniew Brzezinski on the right and the neoconservatives and new rightists on the far right, in the Reagan era we find Young off the chart and Vance on the left. The dominant Republocrat spectrum is sharply skewed to the right. The real left—which proposes a foreign policy based on non-intervention and respect for self-determination—is closed out.

Today's relative "left" is a depleted outpost of traditional liberals such as standard bearer Ted Kennedy (who showed the bankruptcy of liberalism with his support for the Graham-Rudman-Hollings deficit scam), retiring House Speaker Tip O'Neill and beleaguered Geraldine Ferraro. Neoliberals such as Rep. Stephen Solarz and Democratic presidential aspirants Gary Hart and Mario Cuomo (liberal by reputation, neoliberal in practice) are at "center-left." Zbigniew Brzezinski is "center-left" in theory and "centrist" in practice (he supports military aid to the contras, for example). Such "pragmatic conservatives" as Henry Kissinger, Senate Majority leader Robert Dole and Secretary of State George Shultz claim the so-called center, with a heavy lean to the right, apparent in Shultz's anti-terrorist crusade, for example. Vice President George Bush is in the "center," notwithstanding his desperate pandering to the far right which even whiny

## The "Relevant" Policy Spectrum

George Will finds offensive. Says Will: "The unpleasant sound Bush is emitting as he traipses from one conservative gathering to another is a thin, tinny 'arf'—the sound of a lapdog."[3] Defense Secretary Caspar Weinberger is a "center-right" megamilitarist who, heretofore, has liked piling up his weapons more than using them. The right considers him too "pro-Arab"—a legacy of his former employment with the Bechtel Corporation, a multinational construction firm heavily invested in the Middle East—to be one of them.

The right (old, new, neoconservative and fundamentalist) is a crowded place with Reagan himself, Republican presidential hopeful Jack Kemp, *Real American* heroine Jeane Kirkpatrick, "Young Turk" congressional leader Newt Gingrich, Attorney General Ed Meese, etc. Even further out is the far right of Jesse Helms and Jerry Falwell, once considered too extremist to be respectable and relevant, now considered too relevant not to be respected. At a meeting of his reincarnated Liberty Federation, George Bush hailed Falwell: "America is in crying need of the moral vision you will bring to our political life." About the only factions of the right that aren't respectable are neo-Nazis and survivalists dedicated to the violent overthrow of the government. Loyal neo-Nazis, klansmen and average armageddonists are quite welcome.

Speaking about his Administration, Ronald Reagan has said, "Sometimes our right hand doesn't know what our far right hand is doing." So it goes for the relevant foreign policy spectrum.

Dan Wasserman

The elite spectrum offers up three basic foreign policy choices in varying states of confusion: unlimited containment or rollback; moderate or limited containment; and liberal containment. There's agreement across the spectrum that the United States must "draw the line" against perceived threats to U.S. interests. There's disagreement over where, when and how. Virtually everyone (with the notable exception of Gary Hart, to whom we'll return) agrees that the Middle East is an area of vital importance because its oil is considered the "lifeblood" of Western capitalism. (Persian Gulf oil is of greater immediate importance to Western Europe and Japan than the United States, but the region reportedly holds most of the world's untapped oil reserves.)[4] Even on the Middle East, however, policymakers don't agree about how best to police it: e.g. whether and how to station U.S. ground troops permanently in the region; how best to protect the Saudi regime; how to deal with the "Palestinian problem."

The rollbackers rehash their ideas in such organizations as the Committee on the Present Danger, the Hoover Institution and the Heritage Foundation. Their journals include *Commentary* and *National Review*. Proponents of limited containment congregate in the American Enterprise Institute, Georgetown University Center for Strategic and International Studies (CSIS), Council on Foreign Relations (CFR) and the Trilateral Commission, and write for such journals as CSIS's *Washington Quarterly* and the CFR's *Foreign Affairs*. Liberals also belong to the Trilateral Commission and CFR, but their preferred vehicle of expression is *Foreign Policy*, published by the Carnegie Endowment for International Peace.

## Rollback

Unlimited containment is, of course, a contradiction in terms. A more accurate label would be unlimited intervention or rollback. Rollbackers say draw the line everywhere and redraw it in Nicaragua, Angola, Eastern Europe and ultimately the Soviet Union itself. Anything less will mean inevitable American surrender in the ongoing Third World War. In the words of the Committee of Santa Fe* (May 1980):

> World War III is almost over. The Soviet Union, operating under the cover of increasing nuclear superiority, is strangling the Western industrialized nations by interdicting their oil and ore supplies and is encircling the People's Republic of China.
>
> Latin America and Southern Asia are the scenes of strife of the third phase of World War III [the first two phases were containment and detente]...
>
> America is everywhere in retreat. The impending loss of the petroleum of the Middle East and potential interdiction of the sea routes spanning the Indian Ocean, along with the Soviet satellization of the mineral zone of Southern Africa, foreshadow the Finlandization of Western Europe and the alienation of Japan.

* The Committee of Santa Fe was comprised of L. Francis Bouchey, Roger W. Fontaine, David C. Jordan, Gordon Sumner and Lewis Tambs, report editor. Under Reagan, Fontaine became a National Security Council advisor for Latin American affairs, Sumner became a special adviser to Assistant Secretary of State for Inter-American Affairs Thomas Enders and Tambs became ambassador to Colombia.

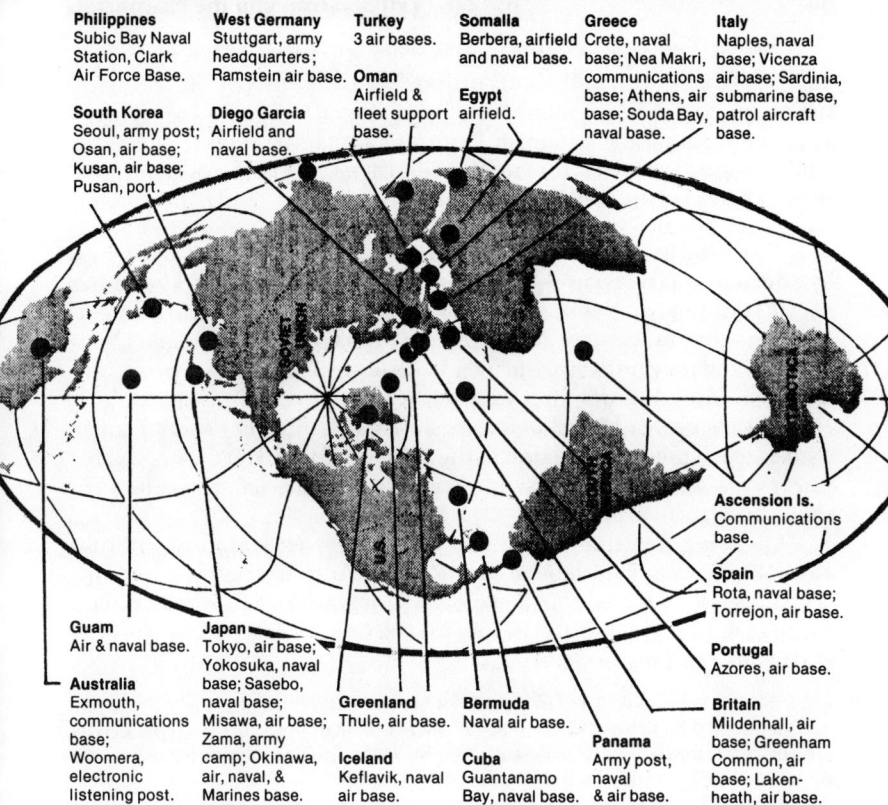

**Philippines**
Subic Bay Naval Station, Clark Air Force Base.

**South Korea**
Seoul, army post; Osan, air base; Kusan, air base; Pusan, port.

**West Germany**
Stuttgart, army headquarters; Ramstein air base.

**Diego Garcia**
Airfield and naval base.

**Turkey**
3 air bases.

**Oman**
Airfield & fleet support base.

**Somalia**
Berbera, airfield and naval base.

**Egypt**
airfield.

**Greece**
Crete, naval base; Nea Makri, communications base; Athens, air base; Souda Bay, naval base.

**Italy**
Naples, naval base; Vicenza air base; Sardinia, submarine base, patrol aircraft base.

**Guam**
Air & naval base.

**Australia**
Exmouth, communications base; Woomera, electronic listening post.

**Japan**
Tokyo, air base; Yokosuka, naval base; Sasebo, naval base; Misawa, air base; Zama, army camp; Okinawa, air, naval, & Marines base.

**Greenland**
Thule, air base.

**Iceland**
Keflavik, naval air base.

**Bermuda**
Naval air base.

**Cuba**
Guantanamo Bay, naval base.

**Panama**
Army post, naval & air base.

**Ascension Is.**
Communications base.

**Spain**
Rota, naval base; Torrejon, air base.

**Portugal**
Azores, air base.

**Britain**
Mildenhall, air base; Greenham Common, air base; Lakenheath, air base.

New York Times

# Military Bases Around the Globe

"Ten years ago there were 323 sizeable installations outside the continental United States, including a few in American territories such as Guam. Today, the total is 359, not including foreign military bases to which American forces have access but not control.

In contrast, the Soviet Union has come but recently to what military officers call power projection and has few military units abroad, save for the massive land and air forces occupying Eastern Europe and the forces that invaded Afghanistan in late 1979. Soviet ships and aircraft are limited to access to bases in countries such as South Yemen, Ethiopia, Vietnam and Cuba..."*

According to **World Military and Social Expenditures 1985,**** the United States has military bases in 40 foreign countries and territories, "supported by an advantage in naval power and a wide-ranging web of alliances." The U.S. has 95,000 military personnel overseas, in addition to 385,000 in NATO Europe and Japan. The Soviet Union has forces in 22 countries and an estimated 23,000 military personnel abroad, in addition to 115,000 fighting in Afghanistan and 640,000 in Warsaw Pact countries.

\* Richard Halloran, **New York Times**, July 24, 1983
\*\* By Ruth Legar Sivard, World Priorities, Washington D.C.

Even the Caribbean, America's maritime crossroad and petroleum refining center, is becoming a Marxist-Leninist lake. Never before has the Republic been in such jeopardy from its exposed southern flank...

It is time to seize the initiative...It is time to sound a clarion call for freedom, dignity and national self-interest which will echo the spirit of the American people. Either a *Pax Sovietica* or a worldwide counter-projection of American power is in the offing. The hour of decision can no longer be postponed.[5]

To the rollbackers, detente is just another word for treason—a plot by multinational corporate "one worlders" out to make a buck, whether in rubles, yen or pesos. Arms control is unilateral disarmament. Accommodation is appeasement. To the rollbackers, the Panama Canal Treaties and the Zimbabwe independence settlement were not new leases on a neocolonial future; they were sellouts.

Rollbackers call for a "new nationalism." U.S. policy should not be moderated to preserve cohesion in the Atlantic Alliance. If the ungrateful Europeans won't go along with Born-Again America, then the U.S. should go-it-alone.

Enduring peaceful coexistence with the Soviet Union is unthinkable. The rollbackers lament the Reagan Administration's lost opportunity to "further a process of disintegration within the Soviet empire" during the Polish crisis of 1981-82. *Commentary* editor Norman Podhoretz explains:

when martial law was declared in Poland...Thanks to the inability of the Poles to pay the interest on their debts to Western banks, there was an opportunity to keep the crisis at a boil by declaring Poland in default. No risk of war was posed by such a policy and yet from the haste with which the United States and even more the West Europeans, shrank from it, one might have thought that they expected the Soviets to launch a nuclear strike if the West refused to roll over the Polish loans.[6]

To the rollbackers the Soviet Union is an evil empire with a master plan for world domination through terrorism, guerrilla warfare and military superiority. U.S. nuclear superiority under Star Wars is seen as necessary and attainable. In the rollbackers' nuclearized crusade to vanquish the Anti-Capitalist, God is on their side.

For many rollbackers, Armageddon is the pre-ordained preface to the Second Coming and its theocracy of Christian believers. Ronald Reagan is the Believer-in-Chief. In 1971, then Governor Reagan remarked:

In the 38th chapter of Ezekiel, it says that the land of Israel will come under attack by the armies of the ungodly nations and it says that Libya will be among them. Do you understand the significance of that? Libya has now gone communist, and that's a sign that the day of Armageddon isn't that far off...Everything is falling into place...Ezekiel tells us that Gog, the nation that will lead all of the other powers of darkness against Israel, will come out of the north...now that Russia has become communist and atheistic, now that Russia has set itself against God. Now it fits the description of Gog perfectly.[7]

In 1983 President Reagan told *People* magazine: "theologians... have said that never...has there ever been a time in which so many of the

## The "Relevant" Policy Spectrum

prophecies are coming together. There have been times in the past when people thought the end of the world was coming and so forth, but never anything like this." In the fundamentalist prophecies of Armageddon, good Christians will be saved from nuclear holocaust and lifted to heaven in the Rapture. Armageddonists don't need to believe Star Wars will provide an impenetrable shield. It just has to help out by buying some time for the Rapture.

**Egostrategics**
When it comes to the Third World, the Ivy League foreign policy Establishment has its geostrategics, epitomized by Henry Kissinger. Rightwingers prefer *Egostrategics*. It's very simple. If you're not for US, you're against US. If you're for US, you're the "moderate autocrat" of a "moderately repressive regime" like Pinochet of Chile, Chun of South Korea, King Fahd of Saudi Arabia, Zia of Pakistan and Mobutu of Zaire (friendly autocrat alumni include Marcos, Duvalier, the Shah and Somoza.) If you're against US, you're a "totalitarian dictator," like Presidents Ortega of Nicaragua and dos Santos of Angola. If you're for US, you're democratic "freedom fighters," like the contras and the Angolan UNITA force headed by Jonas Savimbi. If you're against US, you're Soviet-Libyan-Cuban-backed Marxist-Leninist "terrorists," like the Salvadoran FMLN, South African ANC and Palestine Liberation Organization.

Egostrategists don't accommodate and they don't apologize. Being American means never having to say you're sorry.

"IF YOU SEE THIS MAN ASK HIM WHY HE IS SUBSIDIZING THE KREMLIN'S AFRICAN MILITARY BUILDUP."

Chevron Chairman George Keller, featured on Conservative Caucus campaign literature

At the 1984 Republican convention Jeane Kirkpatrick railed against the Democrats who "always blame America first." Just as former U.N. Ambassador Andrew Young epitomized the congenial Carter *style*, former U.N. Ambassador Jeane Kirkpatrick epitomizes the arrogance and paranoia of Reaganism. A prototypical neoconservative, Kirkpatrick was a partisan of Cold War liberal Hubert Humphrey before becoming a co-founder of the Coalition for a Democratic Majority which opposed George McGovern's candidacy for president in 1972. Neoconservative Democrats merged with rightwing Republicans in the Committee on the Present Danger, founded in 1976 to campaign against detente. Kirkpatrick is a specialist in the disinformation and doublespeak of egostrategics:

> Generally speaking, traditional autocrats tolerate social inequities, brutality and poverty, while revolutionary autocracies create them.
> Traditional autocrats leave in place existing allocations of wealth, power, status and other resources which in most traditional societies favor an affluent few and maintain masses in poverty. But they worship traditional gods and observe traditional taboos. They do not disturb the habitual rhythms of work and leisure, habitual places of residence, habitual patterns of family and personal relations. Because the miseries of traditional life are familiar, they are bearable to ordinary people, who growing up in the society, learn to cope, as children born to untouchables in India acquire the skills and attitudes necessary for survival in the miserable roles they are destined to fill.

"Such societies create no refugees," she adds. Such is the depth of Kirkpatrick's much-acclaimed scholarly knowledge.[8]

In Kirkpatrick's world—enforced by the Immigration and Naturalization Service—refugees from "moderately repressive" regimes are not refugees; they are self-serving fortune seekers. "Ordinary people" don't rebel; they habitually bear their traditional miseries unless the commies stir up trouble. If that happens, the U.S. objective is clear: reinstate order.

# The "Relevant" Policy Spectrum

As Kirkpatrick wrote in a published article, "The problem confronting El Salvador is Thomas Hobbes's problem: How to establish order and authority in a society where there is none."[9] She spells out her draconian views on the solution in an unpublished 1980 paper for the American Enterprise Institute, "The Hobbes Problem: Order, Authority and Legitimacy in Central America":

> Order, as John Stuart Mill emphasizes, is the "preservation of all existing goods."...heroes are people who make a special contribution to highly valued goods.
>
> Hernandez Martinez is such a hero. General Maximiliano Hernandez Martinez, who governed El Salvador from 1931 to 1944, was minister of war in the cabinet of President Arturo Araujo when there occurred widespread uprisings said to be the work of Communist agitators. General Hernandez Martinez then staged a coup and ruthlessly suppressed the disorders—wiping out all those who participated, hunting down their leaders. It is sometimes said that 30,000 persons lost their lives in this process. To many Salvadorans the violence of this repression seems less important than that of the fact of restored order and the thirteen years of civil peace that ensued. The traditional death squads that pursue revolutionary activities and leaders in contemporary El Salvador call themselves Hernandez Martinez Brigades, seeking thereby to place themselves in El Salvador's political tradition and communicate their purposes.[10]

No wonder Kirkpatrick is considered a heroine by the Nicaraguan contras. The "Jeane Kirkpatrick Task Force" is the only contra unit named for a foreigner. "The men chose the name themselves," reports contra leader Adolfo Calero. "They listen to the Voice of America and they admire Mrs. Kirkpatrick for her courage."[11]

Dan Wasserman

## Limited Containment

In the words of Dr. Brzezinski, advocates of limited containment (hereafter known as neointerventionists) reject "nostalgia" for the *Pax Americana* of the 1950s. And they reject the so-called "escapism" of the post-Vietnam seventies.[12] They look back on Nixon-Carter detente as overly optimistic, but look forward to a gradual resumption of a new form of detente.

East-West detente is possible because the Soviets are seen, not as a demonic expansionist empire, but as a more traditional nationalist power, committed to preserving its own security and pragmatic in its attempts to expand its influence where there is relatively low cost and risk involved. A 1983 Trilateral Commission report, *Trilateral Security*, observes:

> The trilateral countries and the Soviet Union stand at a crossroads. They can either reach accommodations which will make possible a reduction of their military competition or face an increasingly unstable world in which the economic burdens of defense will grow and the security of all nations will diminish.[13]

Neointerventionists differ from rollbackers in their assessment of Soviet power. The rollbackers envision U.S.-Soviet competition as a global chess game with novel rules: only Soviet advances matter; when pieces shift from the Soviet side to the U.S. side (e.g. Egypt) you pretend not to notice. Non-aligned countries, needless to say, are considered Soviet pawns. The neointerventionists count perceived wins and losses on both sides. In the trilateralist view:

> While it is appropriate to stress the extent and implications of Soviet military strength, the Soviet Union's weaknesses should not be overlooked. The Soviets are in a sense encircled by nations which are now alarmed by the aggressive nature of the Soviet system. The invasion of Afghanistan has led to a seemingly indefinite military entanglement for the Soviets which is proving costly in men and resources, as well as in its prejudicial impact on world public opinion. The Soviet-sponsored repression in Poland has set back, perhaps for a generation, the Soviet aim of having a stable situation on its Western marches. And to the East, China gives every indication of remaining a strong rival of Soviet influence in Asia and elsewhere. Internally, many observers expect that the stagnation of the Soviet economy will deepen during the decade, and the shifting balance of nationalities will place non-Russians in the majority...[14]

Advocates of limited containment reject a goal of nuclear superiority as destabilizing, unattainable and politically harmful to the Western alliance. They want "multilateralism," shared policies among the allies, not go-it-alone "unilateralism." *Democracy Must Work: A Trilateral Agenda for the Decade*, co-authored by Brzezinski, recommends that the annual economic summits be renamed "Strategic or Policy Summits" to reflect their embrace of a more comprehensive economic, political and military program.[15]

Neointerventionists recognize limits on U.S. power, however reluctantly. Their more limited brand of militarism requires sustainable boosts in military spending (before alarm bells went off on the U.S. budget deficit, the "moderate" range for yearly increased military spending was 3 to 8 percent above inflation). They advocate nuclear modernization (e.g. "Midgetman" missile and stealth bomber) with a "moderate" dose of arms control (e.g. continued support for the ABM Treaty, reductions in intermediate range and intercontinental missiles). Neointerventionists want strengthened conventional forces, effective rapid deployment forces and a possible return to the draft. Some "moderates" support the No-First-Use position advocated by Gerard Smith, chief SALT I negotiator; McGeorge Bundy, former national security adviser; Robert McNamara, former secretary of defense and

# The "Relevant" Policy Spectrum

"We're in luck! A distinguished panel of experts!"  Bob Englehard

World Bank president; and George Kennan, former ambassador to the Soviet Union.[16] Many don't.

Limited containment means limited intervention, but there is no consensus definition. The need to establish priorities outside the "vital" Persian Gulf region is asserted with little elaboration in two important documents associated with the Council on Foreign Relations: *The Soviet Challenge: A Policy Framework for the 1980s*, produced by a Commission on U.S.-Soviet Relations chaired by the editor-in-chief of Time Inc., Henry Grunwald, and *Western Security: What Has Changed? What Should Be Done*, a report prepared jointly by then CFR President Winston Lord (now ambassador to China) and leaders of the British Royal Institute of International Affairs, the German Society for Foreign Affairs and the French Institute of International Relations. *The Soviet Challenge* observes, "As a world power, the United States no doubt has some degree of interest almost anywhere." But the U.S. "cannot and should not involve itself—at least militarily—wherever adverse trends appear."[17]

*Western Security* asserts: "We can also agree to take a relatively relaxed view about a number of so-called 'Marxist' regimes in the Third World whose relationship with the Soviet Union is tenuous and cynical." No examples are given. More problematic, according to the report, "is where the Soviet Union intervenes in a Third World country and threatens its neighbors either though its own military pressure or through surrogates, such as the Cubans or Vietnamese. We have seen in recent years a disturbing series of such interventions in Africa, the Middle East and parts of Asia."[18] Would Central America have been included in the series of alleged interventions if the report had been prepared later? Again, the sweep of interests and allegations is broad, the definition of what is to be done rather abstract.

## Need Versus Want

In 1980, Robert Tucker (professor of International Law and Diplomacy at the Johns Hopkins School of Advanced International Studies, a contributor to *The Soviet Challenge* and president of the conservative Lehrman Institute) proposed a simple rule of moderate containment: the rule of "need" versus "want."

The West "needs" Persian Gulf oil, said Tucker, and thus has a vital interest in countering Soviet moves as well as blocking the admittedly more likely indigenous challenges to the *internal order* of pro-West regimes such as Saudi Arabia. U.S. ground troops should be prepositioned in the region to handle popular rebellions and other non-Soviet threats, and to provide a credible "tripwire" for nuclear force.

Tucker is the type of world-order power broker the ideologues deplore—and government officials don't employ as speechwriters. He recognizes a Soviet claim to its own sphere of influence. Rollback is too dangerous an assault on the post-World War II order. In a piece bluntly titled "Trading Poland for the Gulf," Tucker argues, "The crises in Poland and the Persian Gulf invite comparison not only because in both instances the vital interests of a superpower are at stake but also because in both instances force may have to be employed against movements that enjoy undoubted legitimacy." "In both Poland and the Persian Gulf," says Tucker, "the issue today is above all one of order, not of justice."[19]

In contrast to the Persian Gulf, Central America is a case of "want." Tucker argued that it has no vital resources which make it a legitimate security concern worth the risks of intervention. As Tucker put it: "We have now passed the period of overthrowing an Arbenz in Guatemala [1954], when disposing of governments to which we took offense was a quite easy undertaking."[20]

As Tucker saw it then, the only vital interest in Central America was to prevent the Soviets from developing military relations with Nicaragua or other countries along the lines of Cuba. Otherwise, radical regimes can be tolerated, assuming they can be co-opted through good relations with the U.S.

Cost-benefit containment depends upon shared criteria of vital interests. But there is no consensus about what comprises "need." In the case of natural resources, for example, if oil is the vital resource which gives the U.S. a license to intervene in the Middle East, then what about oil in Mexico and the Caribbean? Where some downplay the strategic importance of southern Africa, others point to its uranium, cobalt and other resources and call it the "Persian Gulf of minerals."

Even on the Middle East, the consensus is not solid. Neoliberal leader Gary Hart registers his emphatic dissent from the Pentagon priority objective of "ensuring access to the oil in Southwest Asia," calling such war preparation a "disgrace to our national honor." Hart asserts, "We never should be reduced to shedding the blood of a single American in an unnecessary war for someone else's oil." It would be futile anyway, he says, given the vulnerability of oil wells and tankers to sabotage and attack. "Instead of relying on the Rapid Deployment Force

to keep oil coming from the Middle East," says Hart, "we need an energy policy that will keep us from sending the RDF after oil."[21] Unfortunately, Hart is an enthusiastic "military reformer" who contributes more ideas to the streamlining and strengthening of U.S. intervention forces—especially "the restoration of United States naval superiority"—than he does to the development of alternatives to military intervention.

Cost-benefit containment becomes even muddier when other political-military considerations are assessed. Regarding Central America, Michael Barnes, neoliberal chairman of the House Subcommittee on Western Hemisphere Affairs and senior counsellor to the Kissinger Commission, says, "The only vital interest of the United States in Central America that most Americans would appear to agree on is the interest in preventing the emplacement of outside military capabilities in the region that could directly threaten the United States."[22]

In a paper for CSIS, Henry Kissinger advocates priorities in U.S. policy, but negates this with his challenge to those who doubt Central America is a vital interest: "Which responsible national leader can risk that experiment? If it is 'vital,' and we make an effort, we may have wasted some resources [not to mention lives]. But if we think it isn't 'vital' and are wrong, we will not have a chance for another experiment."[23]

## The Credibility Quagmire

Alan Tonelson, associate editor of *Foreign Policy*, observes: "U.S. foreign policy from 1945 through the mid-1970s was based largely on [universalist] doctrines and theories, such as the Truman Doctrine, the containment theory and the domino theory, that explicitly held that challenges to America's interests could not be seen in isolation."[24]

In an extreme statement of this view President Reagan declared in his April 1983 address to Congress that if the U.S. cannot defend itself in Central America "we cannot expect to prevail elsewhere. Our credibility would collapse, our alliances would crumble and the safety of our homeland would be put to jeopardy."

In 1980 Robert Tucker had played down the importance of intangible credibility, saying "The eagle that kills the deer in Central America will not frighten the bear in the Middle East."[25] By 1983, however, Tucker gave added significance to the credibility factor:

> Although the sky will not fail if we do not "prevail" in Central America, our defeat there may well entail serious consequences for our broader security interests elsewhere. It is not the safety of shipping lanes, or the prospects of a flood of refugees to this country, or the danger held out to the stability of Mexico that is ultimately at stake in Central America; it is the credibility of United States power.[26]

The real concern is far broader than the credibility of U.S. power vis-a-vis the Soviet Union. It is the credibility of U.S. power in preserving U.S. dominance over the world economy. On El Salvador, Tucker rejected the simple choice between a revolutionary victory and a U.S. military victory, and pointed to the possibility of a third option, commonly known as power-sharing, through which radical sectors could be incorporated into a government which accommodated U.S. concerns and thus preserved U.S credibility. On Nicaragua, he offered only ambiguity.

Tonelson recalls a lesson from King Frederick the Great: he who seeks to defend everything ultimately defends nothing. Besides North America, Western Europe, Japan and the Persian Gulf, priorities would include South Korea, "an important cog in the world economy," whose "security directly affects Japan's" and Egypt, which "has won the right to large amounts of U.S. aid with its post-1977 Middle East diplomacy and its willingness to permit Washington to use Egyptian military facilities to support U.S. fighting forces in the event of a Persian Gulf crisis." (Israel, he says, is less a strategic asset than a moral concern.) Although Tonelson argues "There is hardly any security justification at present for extensive U.S. military or political engagement in the affairs of sub-Saharan Africa, the South and southeastern Pacific, or Latin America"—excluding, for example, the establishment of "a Soviet military base or a local threat to the Panama Canal"—there are many important "cogs in the world economy" whose security is perceived to effect the U.S. or its allies as much as South Korea.[27] The lesson for us is that neointerventionists who seek to defend different priorities differently are locked into a policy quagmire: they can agree more easily upon when to intervene militarily (and paramilitarily), then when not to.

## Liberal Containment

Advocates of liberal containment are the doves in today's Establishment spectrum. They want containment with minimal confrontation with the Soviet Union and maximum accommodation to Third World change. Most convinced of the correctness of the early trilateralist approach, they emphasize the use of reform to preempt or co-opt revolution and preserve Western dominance in its more subtle neocolonial form.

When it comes to nuclear policy, liberals advocate nuclear arms reductions, limits on space weaponry, support for a Comprehensive Test Ban Treaty and progress toward a No-First-Use position. As the Nuclear Weapons Freeze gained public support, prominent liberals such as Ted Kennedy became active sponsors. Many liberal interventionists championed the Freeze, only to undermine it with their support for destabilizing weapons such as the trident, cruise and pershing II missiles. Moreover, most Establishment supporters of the Freeze—liberals and non-liberals alike—would apply their nuclear divestments to the conventional war portfolio.

Robert Legvold, formerly director of the CFR's Soviet Project, set forth a liberal containment approach in a 1980 article titled "Containment without Confrontation." Legvold argued that "An effective Soviet policy must proceed on two tracks":

...one of firmness, military strength (but not by seeking military superiority) and a will to act (requiring a public readied for the possibility); the other of cooperation, the extended hand and a renewed interest in dealing with problems jointly rather than in turning problems against each other.

More specifically, the latter track emphasizes arms control as central to national security policy and calls for cooperation in economic policy and a "serious attempt to open the one area of detente that never got started, namely, crisis management." The military track calls for "a reinstated draft, real progress on NATO's long-term defense program, an effective Rapid Deployment Force and, as lesser priorities, a solution to the vulnerability of land-based intercontinental missiles and a response to new Soviet theatre nuclear weapons," as well as the strengthening of U.S. military power in the Persian Gulf.

Legvold's "containment without confrontation" position is hardly nonconfrontationalist. Like most strategists in the "politically relevant spectrum," he supports military assistance to the Afghan resistance to "draw the line" against such Soviet interventions in the future. He posed a set of rhetorical questions on the nature of U.S. intervention, which unfortunately went unanswered:

What realistic limits are Americans shooting for? The United States will seek to deter further Afghanistans, obviously—that is, no more military invasions to make or save "revolutions." Presumably as well, any further joint Soviet-Cuban expeditions to force the outcome in fluid settings such as Angola are unacceptable. But will Americans oppose support for so-called freedom fighters such as the Patriotic Front in pre-independent Zimbabwe; or intriguing with groups such as the Sandinistas in Nicaragua? Will U.S. policy oppose Soviet intervention even where, in effect, international norms are being upheld, as in the Horn of Africa?[28]

Like Tucker's rule of Need vs. Want, Legvold's questions suggest criteria which even interventionists debate. Take the issue of "international norms." Some would argue, as African leaders do, that Cuban support for the Angolan government does adhere to "international norms": Angola's MPLA government, widely recognized as legitimate by countries other than the United States—not to mention by the U.S. oil companies which are heavily invested there—*invited* Cuban forces to help them resist a South African invasion force which threatened to reach the capital. Does the "obvious" criteria that the U.S. "will seek to deter further Afghanistans" mean that the U.S. would actively block a Soviet intervention in Poland, part of its sphere of influence? Does it mean the U.S. forgoes the right to intervene in its sphere of influence "to make or save" pro-Western capitalist regimes faced with popular rebellion? There is a double standard, of course: the Soviet Union would have no right to "deter further El Salvadors," in the U.S. sphere of influence.

The U.S.-Soviet Panel of the United Nations Association of the U.S.A. (UNA-USA) calls for a strategy similar to Legvold's. (At the time of the report, Cyrus Vance was chairman of the UNA-USA National Council; former U.N. Ambassador William Scranton chaired the panel.) The panel warns that "dynamic indigenous forces for change, such as Islamic nationalism in the Near East, decolonization in Africa and political radicalization in Central America, continue to develop largely beyond Soviet and American control." A successful U.S. policy

requires distinguishing between leftist regimes whose behavior is inimical to Western interests and those with parallel interests; between Soviet-aided but indigenously controlled movements and Soviet-dominated forces lacking genuine roots in the local society; and, finally, between pro-Western regimes whose stable and responsive governments make them potentially reliable partners and those whose days are numbered because they are out of touch with the needs of their own people.[29]

Unfortunately, no examples are given. What would the UNA-USA panel recommend if an indigenous revolution threatened to bring down the current Saudi regime? The panel clearly supports intervention in some cases in the Third World. It singled out the "readiness" of conventional armed forces to carry out missions around the world as the most "important and pervasive weakness" in the U.S. military posture. The familiar key is rapid deployment: "In the 1980s—a decade likely to be characterized by sudden and unpredictable events affecting US interests in distant parts of the world—US forces should be flexible and mobile."

**Accommodation in South Africa**

An accommodationist program for South Africa was proposed in the lengthy May 1981 report, *South Africa: Time Running Out*. The report was prepared by an independent Study Commission on U.S. Policy Toward Southern Africa, sponsored by the Rockefeller Foundation and chaired by Ford Foundation President Franklin Thomas.

Events have outpaced *Time Running Out*, but its recommendations posed a distinct alternative to the Reagan brand of "constructive engagement" and illustrate the parameters of accommodation. According to the Commission, the U.S. has the following basic interests in South Africa:

1. Protecting U.S. military and strategic interests and minimizing Soviet influence in Southern Africa.
2. Ensuring adequate supplies of key minerals imported from South Africa.
3. Advancing political freedom and civil liberties for all South Africans.
4. Maintaining satisfactory diplomatic and commercial relations with other African countries.
5. Maintaining commercial relations with South Africa.[30]

Not surprisingly, the Commission rejected economic disinvestment. It suggested that "U.S. corporations and financial institutions operating in South Africa should commit themselves [voluntarily] to a policy of nonexpansion and those businesses not already there should not enter the country." (That sounds more like an anti-competition policy than an anti-apartheid policy.) A "generous proportion of corporate resources—determined in accordance with a specific 'social development expenditure standard'—should be set aside to improve the lives of black South Africans." Also, "U.S. companies that have not yet subscribed to the Sullivan Principles [which purport to challenge apartheid by improving Black wages and working conditions] should do so and companies would be effectively monitored." While ruling out disinvestment and a trade embargo at that time, the Commission did note that "Trade embargoes and disinvestment remain legitimate instruments of policy" for circumstances of "widespread violence, massive repression, or civil war." Presumably, an Administration following Commission policy would have endorsed a trade embargo sooner than Reagan was forced to. But, it is unlikely the Commission would have admitted the hypocrisy of the Sullivan Principles approach and endorsed comprehensive disinvestment.

In contrast to the Reagan policy of constructive engagement, the Commission supported "the exclusion of South Africa from full membership in the Western community of nations" until "Blacks have obtained an effective share in political power." And unlike Reagan, the Commission would demonstrate "that it does not accept the view that South Africa, under its white minority government, is a bulwark against Communism." Rather, it "sees apartheid as a target and an opportunity for the growth of Communist influence in the region." The Commission advocated broadening the arms embargo to cover foreign subsidiaries of U.S. companies as well as broadening the embargo on nuclear collaboration with South Africa.

In the Commission's view the "choice" in South Africa was "not between 'slow peaceful change' and 'quick violent change' but between a slow, uneven, sporadically violent evolutionary process and a slow but much more violent descent into civil war." The report depicted two scenarios to illuminate this choice, noting they are not mutually exclusive. In the first scenario, Pretoria is both reformist and careful to "select its targets for repression."

The pattern would probably be one of increasingly forceful black demands, cautious and limited white concessions, increased black capabilities, more black demands, more white concessions and so on, until a new, more just and more viable political order emerged. Eventually, whites would see it in their interest to concede some of their power and blacks would regard it in their interest to not demand all of it.

The premise is that the African National Congress's campaign would be contained; the ANC would not become a viable political force and a multiracial government would emerge, probably with a federal structure allowing much local autonomy (presumably with "moderates" such as Chief Gatsha Buthelezi playing a key role).

In the second scenario, the hardline Afrikaners block government reforms; guerrilla struggle and non-violent forms of struggle escalate; repression is more sweeping; attempts to co-opt Black moderates go on, but the "liberation movements" acquire more popular legitimacy. The Soviet Union and Cuba cautiously increase their support for liberation forces, but Western nations are restrained by domestic and international politics from supporting Pretoria's reactionary policy. South Africa uses economic pressure and military raids against the neighboring "Frontline States" and the United Nations imposes some form of mandatory economic sanctions. "In the end," says the report, "the South African government's belief in victory would collapse, leading to de facto partition or a Zimbabwean type of power-sharing arrangement" (the Zimbabwe settlement produced a Black majority government with guarantees for white minority representation, disproportionately greater than their actual population, and prohibitions against expropriation of white farms to provide land for Blacks who have been deprived of it.)

The Commission preferred the former scenario, but the U.S. could live with the latter one because even though the ANC's role in the liberation struggle would earn it a place in a post-Civil War government, South Africa would probably continue to "export minerals to the West, its natural market." And however close such a government became with the Soviet Union, East Germany and Cuba, it would "probably not compromise its hard-won sovereignty by granting the Soviet Union military base rights."[31]

In the foreward to the new edition of *Time Running Out*, Franklin Thomas applauds the "heightened awareness" about South Africa in the United States and praises a growing "commitment of the South African business community to an equitable society." He advocates negotiations which would preempt the radicalization of younger Black leaders, on the one hand, and Afrikaner intransigence on the other. The "last, best hope for a peaceful reconstruction of governance," says Thomas, "lies in restoring legitimacy to those leaders" suppressed in the past—notably ANC leader Nelson Mandela.[32]

### Accommodation in Central America

On Central America the accommodationist approach is being promoted by the Inter-American Dialogue, a group of political, academic, business, labor and religious leaders from the U.S., Canada, Latin America and the Caribbean who have been meeting since 1982. The Dialogue's co-chairs are Sol Linowitz, chief negotiator for the Panama Canal Treaties and former U.S. ambassador to the Organization of American States (OAS), and Galo Plaza, formerly president of Ecuador and secretary general of the OAS. Among the Dialogue members from the United States are Franklin Thomas, Cyrus Vance, Robert McNamara, McGeorge Bundy, former Secretary of Defense Elliot Richardson, Time Inc. Chairman Ralph Davidson, University of Notre Dame President Theodore Hesburgh, IBM World Trade Americas Chairman Ralph Pfeiffer, Vice President of the Amalgamated Textile and Clothing Workers Union Joyce Miller, San Antonio Mayor Henry Cisneros and Rockefeller Foundation Chairman Clifton Wharton.

In the second Dialogue report, *The Americas in 1984: A Year for Decisions* (a third report is being prepared at this writing), participants argue that the exaggeration of the East-West dimension to events in the regions "has a self-fulfilling quality, for it escalates the level of superpower involvement and confrontation." It warns against a self-created "credibility trap" of "drawing artificial lines that then need to be defended."

### Reagan, Trilateralism and the Neoliberals

Dan Wasserman

Dialogue members assume that the U.S. and other nations in the hemisphere have a "security interest in keeping Soviet and Cuban combat forces and military bases out of Central America and in preventing Cuba and the Soviet Union from disrupting the sea lanes in and around the region." To disentangle Central America from the East-West conflict, reciprocal commitments should be sought regarding combat forces and military bases.

The Dialogue calls for support of the Contadora initiative (sponsored by Mexico, Venezuela, Panama and Colombia). In the context of a Contadora-backed regional accord, the U.S. "should make it clear to the Soviet Union that any attempt by the USSR to introduce combat forces, bases, offensive weapons, or strategic facilities into the Caribbean Basin would be regarded as a serious provocation, calling for the measures necessary to prevent or reverse it." This Dialogue report was written before the MiGs crisis of Fall 1984 discussed in the next chapter. One can only presume that Dialogue members do not mean this as a license to the Reagan Administration to "take out the MiGs" if Nicaragua chooses to import them in the absence of a Contadora accord and in the face of contra warfare.

Regarding Nicaragua, the U.S. "should immediately end support for the military and paramilitary activities of the contras." They contend, "Although some of us think that past pressures may have influenced Nicaragua to be more conciliatory, we believe that further support for them is unjustifiable. It would be ineffective, counter-productive and, in the view of most of us, plain wrong." Written before the November 1984 Nicaraguan election, the report urged the Nicaraguan government and

# The "Relevant" Policy Spectrum

opposition groups to lay the basis for "truly fair, internationally-observed elections."

On El Salvador, says the report, the struggle must be moved "from the battlefield to the political arena" (the Zimbabwe model). Elections "without prior negotiations among the belligerents are not enough. Elections alone do not make effective democracies; democracies make effective elections."

The report also recommends that Cuba and the U.S. open a dialogue on Central America, relying first perhaps upon Contadora intermediaries. "It may be that an opportunity exists for a mutually acceptable resolution of Cuban-U.S. differences over Central America on the basis of a shared interest in de-escalating the conflict."[33]

## Reagan Doctrine

### Shultz vs. Weinberger?

Within the Reagan Administration — which Podhoretz and other rollbackers see as dominated in *practice* by advocates of moderate containment—there has been a public debate over guidelines for military intervention between Secretary of State Shultz and Secretary of Defense Weinberger. In a speech to the Trilateral Commission in April 1984, Shultz argued:

Over twenty years ago, President John Kennedy pledged that the United States would "pay any price, bear any burden, meet any hardship, support any friend, oppose any foe, in order to assure the survival and success of liberty."

"And Remember, We're Here to Defend the National Security of the United States."

Roger

...We know now that we are not omnipotent and that we must set priorities. We cannot "pay *any* price" or "bear *any* burden." We must discriminate...we must respond in ways appropriate to the challenge and engage our power only when very important strategic stakes are involved.[34]

However, in a February 1985 speech to the Commonwealth Club of San Francisco, Shultz committed U.S. support to the so-called "democratic revolution" sweeping the world, and praised the "freedom fighters" of Afghanistan, Cambodia, Ethiopia, Angola, Poland and Nicaragua. Shultz has become increasingly outspoken in his calls for an "active defense" against terrorism directed at the U.S. and its allies. In an October 1984 speech, Shultz asserted:

We may never have the kind of evidence that can stand up in an American court of law [not to mention the World Court]. But we cannot allow ourselves to become the Hamlet of nations, worrying endlessly over whether and how to respond...Fighting terrorism will not be a clean or pleasant contest, but we have no choice but to play it.[35]

Weinberger's pivotal speech in the intervention debate was his November 28, 1984 address to the National Press Club, in which he spelled out six tests for the commitment of U.S. troops: the stakes should be "vital"; there should be a "clear intention of winning"; the forces should be commensurate with "clearly defined political and military objectives"; there should be some reasonable assurance of "popular and congressional support"; and U.S. forces should be a "last resort."

Weinberger's concern about winnability as a primary determinant of U.S. military intervention is not new. During his 1980 confirmation hearings, Weinberger reflected on the lessons of the Vietnam War and asserted that the U.S. should not commit troops to

a war that is not vital for our national security to enter and we should never enter a war that we do not intend to win or in which we do not expend every single effort of every weapon and every facility that we have to win.
...Once we entered it [Vietnam], it became a war that we should have won.[36]

Weinberger's overwhelming priority is to keep the U.S. military buildup on track. From the beginning, he has cautioned against fueling public and congressional opposition with direct, massive military intervention anywhere it was not cheap and quick. This has meant a yellow then green light on Grenada, a red light on Lebanon and a yellow light on Nicaragua and El Salvador. In Central America, the yellow light is edging toward green as the infrastructure for military intervention is solidified, public pretexts for intervention are consolidated and options fade (negotiation is not an Administration option).

This does not mean, as has often been asserted, that State and Defense have reversed roles, with Weinberger acting more like a dove and Shultz acting more like a hawk. That view is misleading. For example, Weinberger is a staunch opponent of arms control agreements with the Soviet Union while Shultz is an advocate of flexible negotiations. Weinberger unequivocally supports the overthrow of the Nicaraguan government while, at least until the latter part of 1985, Shultz attempted to find space in the Administration for a possible political settlement.

## The "Relevant" Policy Spectrum

Weinberger resisted Shultz's view that Marcos was a liability until there was near-unanimous support in Congress and the Administration for the failing dictator's removal.

The goal of Weinberger's military program is to consolidate the ability of the United States to unilaterally wage global war—and win. Weinberger's *relentless military buildup*, to use a term normally reserved for the Soviets (although, according to the CIA's own inflated estimates, the Soviets have increased military spending by a *relatively* small 2 percent in the last two years[37] while the U.S. has averaged nearly 7 percent in yearly increases since 1981) includes expanded Special Forces for counterinsurgency, a 600-ship Navy for modern Gunboat Diplomacy, deployment of first-strike nuclear weapons such as the cruise missile and development of Star Wars to shield the U.S. from Soviet retaliation after a U.S. first-strike.

Continued naval superiority would allow the U.S. to "control the sea lanes" and discard the so-called "one-and-a-half" or "two-and-a-half" war strategies for a "multitheatre" or "global war" strategy which envisions protracted conventional wars in the Third World, lasting many years, and simultaneous warfare with the Soviet Union. The Soviet Union only launched their *first* full-scale aircraft carrier in 1986 and has *begun* building a second; the first carrier, capable of launching some types of fighter planes, will not be fully operational for another 10 years.[38] The integrated conventional-nuclear battlefield would span the globe: the U.S. would confront the Soviets with *vertical escalation*, escalating from conventional to nuclear war, and *horizontal escalation*, attacking not just in the immediate conflict area, but anywhere in the world where the U.S. perceives an advantage. A U.S.-Soviet clash in the Middle East, for example, might bring on a U.S. strike against Cuba.

### Low-Intensity Conflict

Behind the ongoing Shultz-Weinberger debate is a consensus within the Reagan Administration about the preferred mode of military intervention: the so-called Low-Intensity Conflict Doctrine. Low-intensity conflict (LIC) includes guerrilla warfare, terrorism, coups, revolution, border skirmishes, civil war and counterinsurgency campaigns short of full-scale war. Military analyst Michael Klare explains that the LIC designation applies to the current level of fighting in Afghanistan, Angola, Cambodia, Lebanon, the Philippines and Central America. "According to Pentagon strategists," notes Klare, "the Vietnam War fell into the L.I.C. category for most of its duration, though with the massive U.S. air attacks on the North and the invasion of Cambodia, it escalated to a higher level, to 'mid-intensity conflict.'"[39]

The Heritage Foundation report, *Mandate for Leadership II*, describes Reagan Administration initiatives in the three basic areas of low-intensity warfare:

1) countering Marxist insurgencies against friendly governments—the U.S. Army 1st Special Operations Command (SOCOM) and the Joint Chiefs of Staff (JCS) Special Operations Agency (JSOA) were established to respond to low-intensity threats, especially those requiring a counter-insurgency strategy (e.g. El Salvador); 2) assisting pro-Western insurgencies against Marxist regimes—paramilitary assets of the CIA have been expanded to assist insurgents challenging Soviet-backed regimes (e.g. Nicaragua); and 3) negating the threat of terrorism—important initiatives have been undertaken. Presidential National Security Decision Directive (NSDD) 138 ordered the appropriate agencies to develop an offensively focused anti-terrorist capability.[40]

The Heritage report recommends that the Reagan Administration establish a special group to oversee LIC within the National Security Council, and advocates continued or new aid to insurgencies in Cambodia, Angola, Afghanistan, Nicaragua, Laos, Vietnam, Ethiopia, Iran and Libya.

While LIC is the preferred form of military intervention, it is not necessarily a viable strategy for the long run. Precisely because the "freedom fighters" are often more popular in Washington than in their homelands, they have little chance of taking power without more massive U.S. military intervention. LIC is a war of attrition, designed not for rapid overthrow of the targeted regime, but slow-motion destabilization, first of the progressive program, eventually of the "enemy" government itself. But it is unlikely that the U.S. will sustain multiple, perpetual wars of attrition without ever committing its own forces in an attempt to win. Too much "credibility" will be at stake in too many places. Too many doors to escalation—planned or unplanned— will lie open.

At some point, the U.S. may decide that the target regime has been "softened" up sufficiently to go for an invasion. The prevailing Administration assessment of military involvement in Nicaragua is that the U.S. could "quickly and easily rout the Sandinistas." In the words of an important intelligence official, it would be "like falling off a log."[41] Attrition works both ways. To use the language of the relevant spectrum, Congress may "tire" of a seemingly no-win conflict and force a choice between "cutting losses and getting out"—unilaterally or through negotiations—and making a commitment to win. After six years of LIC in Nicaragua, the U.S. has not reached this crossroads, but it is looming nearer. It is to the Nicaraguan example we now turn.

# THE NICARAGUA EXAMPLE

To those imprisoned in regimes held captive, to those beaten for daring to fight for freedom and democracy—for their right to worship, to speak, to live and prosper in the family of free nations—we say to you tonight: you are not alone freedom fighters. America will support with moral and material assistance your right not just to fight and die for freedom, but to fight and win freedom—in Afghanistan; Angola; Cambodia; and Nicaragua.

This is a great moral challenge for the entire free world. Surely, no issue is more important for peace in our own hemisphere, for the security of our frontiers, for the protection of our vital interests—than to achieve democracy in Nicaragua and to protect Nicaragua's democratic neighbors.

President Reagan, State of the Union, 1986

We are proud to be Nicaraguans. This revolution transcends national boundaries. Our revolution has always been internationalist, ever since Sandino fought in the Segovias...

*This does not mean that we export our revolution. It is enough*—and we couldn't do otherwise—*for us to export our example*, the example of the courage, sensitivity, and determination of our people...

How could we not be upset about the injustices that are committed in different parts of the world? But we know that it is the people themselves of these countries who must make their revolution, and we know that by advancing our revolution we are also helping our brothers and sisters in the rest of Latin America. (Emphasis added.)

Tomas Borge, The Second Anniversary of the Sandinista Revolution
July 19, 1981[1]

Following the 1984 vice-presidential debate, George Bush's press secretary told reporters: "You can say anything you want in a debate, and 80 million people hear it. If reporters then document that a candidate spoke untruthfully, so what? Maybe 200 people read it, or 2,000 or 20,000."[2]

The press secretary knows that it's the immediate impact that really counts, not the finer print debates which may follow. Reporters, Congress and the public tend to believe first—or act like they do—and doubt later, no matter how often the "untruths" are documented. (Even in exceptional cases, such as Watergate, the credibility damage is contained and powerful habitual liars, like Kissinger, are lionized or, like Nixon, are restored as respected statesmen.) If a rebuttal is forthcoming in the media, it generally gets far less coverage than the initial headline story—mainly in print, off the front page, with little or nothing on network evening news. The Reagan media strategists, says Jack Nelson of the *Los Angeles Times*, "realize that the first impressions are lasting impressions, that's part of their public relations genius." Grenada, he says, is the "perfect example":

> There are still people who think that place was crawling with armed Cubans. It doesn't matter how often you go back and say that the fact is there were only 500 or 600 Cubans, that you got the truth out of Havana and lies out of Washington, people just say, "Aw, that's just the press."[3]

What's more, the rebuttals are often systematically forgotten in future stories which regurgitate the official line: e.g. the U.S. invaded Grenada at the behest of other Caribbean nations concerned about their security, rescued American students and liberated the Grenadian people. If any doubts remain about U.S. justifications for invading, no matter; the Grenadian people love us for it. In the words of a *New York Times* editorial, on the occasion of Reagan's February 20, 1986 visit to the island: "America's political conduct since then has been wholly admirable" and, notwithstanding the island's grave economic problems which the U.S. will paternalistically help solve, Reagan, "America's conquering hero," deserves to "revel in some merited acclaim."

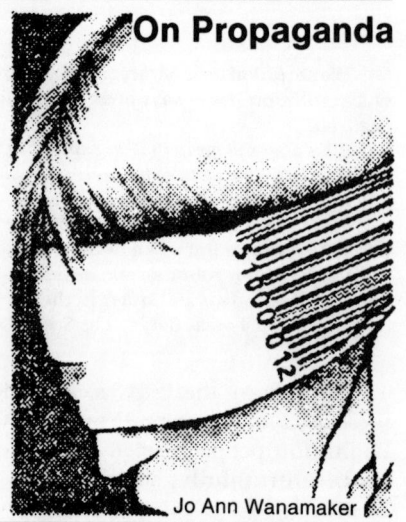

**On Propaganda**

"I have the greatest admiration for your propaganda. Propaganda in the West is carried on by experts who have had the best training in the world—in the field of advertising—and have mastered the techniques with exceptional proficiency... Yours are subtle and persuasive; ours are crude and obvious...

I think that the fundamental difference between our worlds, with respect to propaganda, is quite simple. You tend to believe yours... and we tend to disbelieve ours."

A Soviet correspondent, based five years in the United States, quoted by Farley Mowat in **The Siberians**.

Jo Ann Wanamaker

Ronald Reagan is a "Great Communicator" largely because he understands that "you can say anything you want" and, even better, show "anything you want" in a carefully staged photo opportunity and, "if reporters then document that [you] spoke untruthfully, so what?" Indeed, Reagan's special charm is that the more he "misspeakes," the less his "misstatements" effect his credibility.

Sometimes Reagan "misspeakes" out of ignorance, other times on purpose. The latter is disinformation. Disinformation works best when the media and the public have historical amnesia, short attention spans, ethnocentric educations and an ideological predisposition to believe presidential propaganda. The beauty of disinformation is that the more people are already disinformed, the more receptive they are to being further disinformed.

I'll make one parallel here with the Vietnam War. When J. William Fulbright, the former chairman of the Senate Foreign Relations Committee who changed from being a supporter of the war to a leading critic, was asked to comment on the lessons of Vietnam, he replied, "not to trust Government statements." Referring to government statements on Vietnam and Central America, Fulbright added, "They fit the facts to fit the policy. We made a great mistake in Vietnam and are making another one in Central America."[4]

So it goes with Nicaragua. Fitting the facts to fit the policy—the policy of intervention.

President Reagan has called Nicaragua a "totalitarian dungeon"; the Sandinistas are "infinitely worse than Somoza," he says. He has branded Nicaragua an "outlaw state," part of "a confederation of terrorist states," also including Iran, Libya, North Korea and Cuba. He told the American Bar Association these "outlaw states" were "run by the strangest collection of misfits, Looney Tunes and squalid criminals since the advent of the Third Reich"; the esteemed lawyers laughed and applauded loudly.[5] The formerly more reserved George Shultz has taken to referring to the Nicaraguan government as "a cancer, right here on our land mass."[6] Nicaragua is *our* piece of real estate. The Sandinistas are trespassing; the penalty is vilification and death.

America's Watch, an internationally-respected human rights organization, comments on Reagan policy toward Nicaragua: "It may well be that this tiny country of fewer than three million people has been the target of more criticism on human rights grounds from the Reagan Administration—and especially from the president himself—than any other country in the world."[7] More than South Africa, more than Turkey, more than Chile, maybe even more than the so-called "Evil Empire," the Soviet Union itself. In a report analyzing Reagan rhetoric and reality, America's Watch says the "description of a totalitarian state bears no resemblance to Nicaragua in 1985."

In Nicaragua there is no systematic practice of forced disappearances, extrajudicial killings or torture—as has been the case with the "friendly" armed forces of El Salvador. While prior censorship has been imposed by emergency legislation, debate on major social political questions is robust, outspoken, even often strident. The November 1984 elections, though deficient, were a democratic advance over the past five years of Nicaraguan history and compare favorably with those of El Salvador and Guatemala...Moreover, some notable reductions in abuses [specifically, toward the Miskito Indians] have occurred in Nicaragua since 1982, despite the pressure caused by escalating external attacks.[8]

## The Right to Intervene

The debate over Nicaragua has become more and more one-sided. In Congress, the question isn't whether to intervene in Nicaragua, but how best to intervene. The conservatives yell, "They're the devil." With few exceptions, the liberals respond, "They're devilish, but!" The typical "but" centers upon the concern that the contras can't succeed. An editorial in the February 13, 1985 *New York Times* illustrates this point well. I quote it at length because it epitomizes the narrowness of the debate and the arrogance of U.S. policy, even in its accommodationist form.

President Reagan has given interviewers from The Times a clear, concise statement of his attitude toward the Sandinista rulers of Nicaragua. They betrayed the revolution that Americans cheered for its promise of democracy, he said. They have become pro-Soviet, chased democrats into exile and refused to subject their power to the consent of the Nicaraguan people. The exile army of "contras," therefore, has every reason to fight for democracy. The United States has ample reason to help them.

The President's premises are admirable and accurate. But his attitude is not a policy...Why not?

First, because the costs of exporting democracy by war are usually too high...

A second reason is that we're rotten at making intrusive war, overtly or covertly. The Sandinistas and Fidel Castro are good examples of how rotten. Their regimes result directly from dictatorships sponsored by America's Marines or meddling diplomats...

A third reason is more abstract but no less compelling. Americans don't want to live in a world where nations feel free to impose their political doctrines on others by force. War should be a last resort, to defend vital national interests...

The American-sponsored contra army is simply too weak to overthrow the Sandinistas. Its hit-and-run assaults can damage their economy and punish their hostility. But such warfare also invites either unthinkable escalation or the ultimate humiliation of failing to achieve our stated purpose. Meanwhile the combat cruelly

# The Nicaragua Example

exploits Nicaraguan patriots whose goal we know to be unattainable...

Still, couldn't the contra army hurt the Sandinistas enough to make them willing to deal? Perhaps, if the price were clear to them, and tolerable...What they might do under pressure is agree to bar Soviet and Cuban military bases and to let an inter-American force guard against arms shipments to El Salvador.

What then of the political, religious and labor freedoms that the President and all Americans want to see in Nicaragua? As in dealing with other countries, these could be made the price of real friendship, of aid and trade concessions.

The policy choices in Nicaragua are not between blind force and abject acquiescence. Geography and circumstance create an American interest in Nicaragua's future and opportunities to influence it. Surely judicious pressures for negotiable ends promise a better result than aimless combat. At worst, the Nicaraguan people would be left in a grim peace. At best, they would have America to thank for a gradual improvement in their condition.

> The U.S. is making war on Nicaragua. It is a bloody war, not a war of abstract "pressures" and "punishments" to make the Sandinistas cry "uncle"—as if the Nicaraguan people were so many arms to be twisted behind their government's back. By better understanding this war and the debate which attends it, we can work more effectively to end the war and challenge the interventionist logic which supports it.
>
> I want to make two points at the outset: First, U.S. intervention in Nicaragua is the rule, not the exception. It is not a reluctant response to alleged Sandinista aggression. It has been going on long before the Sandinistas and the Somozas. Moreover, this intervention conforms to an unbroken pattern of U.S. intervention to destabilize all genuinely progressive governments in the hemisphere and much of the world. (See box on intervention below.) To say that Nicaraguans are provoking U.S. intervention is like saying women provoke rape.
>
> Second, the outcome the U.S. fears most in Nicaragua is not a so-called Cuban-style Soviet colony, but a non-aligned, democratic government which delivers on its promises of social justice. Why? Because if it could happen in Nicaragua, it could happen elsewhere, presenting a cumulative challenge to U.S. dominance of Latin America, the Caribbean and the global economy. A Nicaraguan "third way"— neither Soviet-style, nor U.S.-style—would undermine the Cold War logic which is used to justify U.S. intervention in the Third World and keep the Western allies in line.
>
> In 1829, the Latin American liberator Simon Bolivar wrote that the United States "seem destined to plague America to misery in the name of liberty." For Nicaraguans, fear of a U.S. invasion is not rooted in paranoia, but in history. Indeed, according to Karl Bermann, the 1910 overthrow of Nicaragua's nationalist Liberal President Zelaya, was the first occasion anywhere of U.S. intervention to remove an established government.[9]
>
> Earlier, Nicaraguans saw the Tennessee adventurer and slavery advocate William Walker shoot his way into power in 1855 and receive diplomatic recognition from the U.S. In 1912 thousands of marines came ashore to prop up the subservient government of Adolfo Diaz, of the Conservative Party. U.S. officials and bankers directly managed Nica-

ragua's economy, foreign policy and electoral frauds for the next decade. The marines left in 1925, but were back again in 1927 to put down a Liberal rebellion.

The Russian Revolution of 1917 gave Washington a bogeyman to use in scaring up support for its well-worn policy of intervention. In the late 1920s, U.S. officials testified to Congress with supposed evidence of Bolshevist designs on Nicaragua and the Panama Canal. Mexico was then the Russian proxy in subversion. Secretary of State Frank Kellogg claimed that "The Bolshevik leaders have had very definite ideas with respect to the role which Mexico and Latin America are to play in their general program of world revolution." Latin America and Mexico, he asserted, "are conceived as a base for activity against the United States."[10]

In 1927, Under-Secretary of State Robert Olds called Nicaragua a "test case" of U.S. prestige and resolve in a confidential—and thus more candid—memorandum:

## Selected U.S. Military and CIA Interventions

| | |
|---|---|
| 1898-1902 | occupation of Cuba |
| 1899-1902 | Philippines |
| 1901 | "acquires" Puerto Rico |
| 1906-09 | occupation of Cuba |
| 1909 | Nicaragua, overthrow of Zelaya |
| 1912-25 | occupation of Nicaragua |
| 1914 | Mexico |
| 1914-34 | occupation of Haiti |
| 1916-24 | occupation of Dominican Republic |
| 1917-23 | occupation of Cuba |
| 1919 | occupation of Honduran ports |
| 1926-33 | occupation of Nicaragua |
| 1947-49 | Greece |
| 1953 | Iran, overthrow of Mossadeq |
| 1954 | Guatemala, overthrow of Arbenz |
| 1958 | Lebanon |
| 1961 | Bay of Pigs invasion of Cuba |
| 1961-75 | Vietnam, Laos, Cambodia |
| 1964 | Brazil, overthrow of Goulart |
| 1965 | Indonesia |
| 1965-66 | occupation of Dominican Republic |
| 1973 | Chile, overthrow of Allende |
| 1974-76 | Angola |
| 1979 | El Salvador |
| 1980 | Nicaragua |
| 1983 | occupation of Grenada |
| 1985 | Cambodia |
| 1986 | Angola |

Alaska: bought f Russia 1867

Midway: 1945

Hawaii annexe 1898

Philippines: taken from Spain 1898

Marshalls: 1945

Various Pacific Islands: 1945

Primary Source: Jenny Pearce, **Under the Eagle** (Boston: South End Press, 1982)

# The Nicaragua Example

The Central American area down to and including the isthmus of Panama constitutes a legitimate sphere of influence for the United States...Our ministers accredited to the five little republics, stretching from the Mexican border to Panama...have been advisers whose advice has been accepted virtually as law in the capitals where they respectively reside...We do control the destinies of Central America and we do so for the simple reason that the national interest absolutely dictates such a course...Until now Central America has always understood that governments which we recognize and support stay in power, while those which we do not recognize and support fall. Nicaragua has become a test case.

The 1928 Republican Platform said the same thing in language more suited for public consumption:

The United States has an especial interest in the advancement and progress of all the Latin American countries...The marines, now in Nicaragua, are there to protect American lives and property and to aid in carrying out an agreement whereby we have undertaken to do what we can to restore and maintain order and insure a free and fair election. Our policy absolutely repudiates any idea of conquest or exploitation, and is

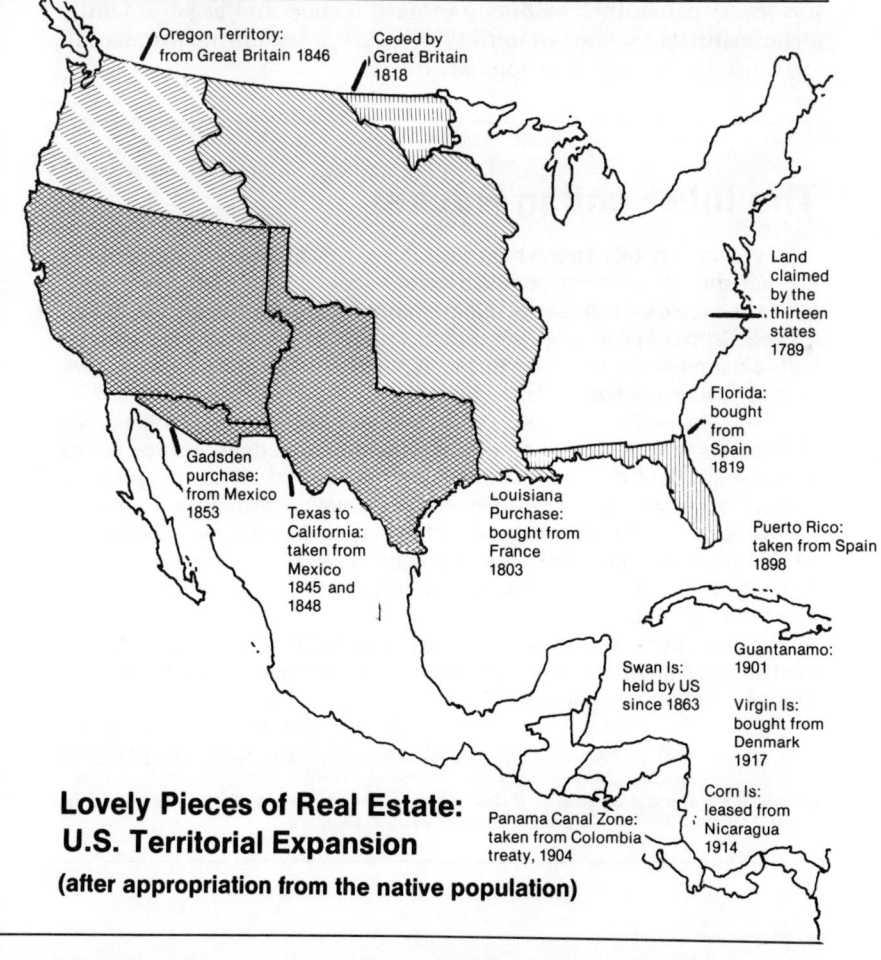

**Lovely Pieces of Real Estate: U.S. Territorial Expansion**
**(after appropriation from the native population)**

actuated solely by an earnest and sincere desire to assist a friendly and neighboring state which has appealed for aid in a great emergency.[11]

Nicaragua's national hero, Augusto Cesar Sandino, rebelled against manifest U.S. control of Central American destiny. He rejected the U.S. attempt to impose a tweedle-dee, tweedle-dum two-party system on Nicaragua with the 1927 Liberal-Conservative peace settlement. Washington called him a "bandit" and an "outlaw." Sandino's genuine freedom fighters raised enough sympathy and caused enough U.S. casualties to fuel an opposition movement in the United States to the Nicaragua intervention then being managed by President Coolidge. The U.S. decided on a longer-range plan to replace U.S. troops and built up the Nicaraguan National Guard. In 1932 Anastasio Somoza Garcia (of the so-called Liberal Party) became the *Guardia* commander, and in 1933 the last U.S. marines left Nicaragua after the U.S-orchestrated elections of 1932. Sandino signed a peace treaty with President Juan Sacasa, but tensions mounted with Somoza's National Guard and in 1934 Sandino was assassinated. In 1936 Somoza staged a coup and began a family dictatorship that was to last until 1979 when the Sandinistas (founded in 1961) overthrew Anastasio Somoza, Jr.

## The Intervention Racket

"War is a racket...It may seem odd for me, a military man, to adopt such a comparison. Truthfulness compels me to. I spent 33 years and 4 months in active service as a member of our country's most agile military force—the Marine Corps...And during the period I spent most of my time being a high-class muscle man for Big Business, for Wall Street and for the bankers. In short, I was a racketeer for capitalism...

Thus I helped make Mexico and especially Tampico safe for American oil interests in 1914. I helped make Haiti and Cuba a decent place for the National City Bank boys to collect revenues in. I helped in the raping of half a dozen Central American republics for the benefit of Wall Street...I helped purify Nicaragua for the international banking house of Brown Brothers in 1909-1912. I brought light to the Dominican Republic for American sugar interests in 1916. I helped make Honduras "right" for American fruit companies in 1903...

Looking back on it, I feel I might have given Al Capone a few hints. The best **he** could do was to operate his racket in three city districts. We Marines operated on three **continents**." [Emphasis original.]

—Major General Smedley D. Butler,
two-time winner of the Congressional Medal of Honor.

Source: Major General Smedley D. Butler, "America's Armed Forces," Parts I and II, **Common Sense,** October 1935; original articles provided by John Lamperti.

# The Nicaragua Example

## Forgotten Gambits

There is a popular myth—perpetuated by liberals and rollbackers alike—which blames U.S. hostility on Sandinista duplicity toward a benevolent Carter Administration. The story goes that Carter paved the Sandinista path to power by withdrawing support from Somoza and then welcomed them with open arms and aid in the first year after the revolution. The bad Sandinistas, we are told, bit the Carter Administration hand that was feeding them by running guns for the Soviets to the Salvadoran revolutionaries. So goes the story. Here's the reality.

By mid 1978, popular rebellion against Somoza had grown to the point that Carter officials felt there was no way to prevent a Sandinista victory *and* keep Somoza in power. As Robert Pastor, Carter's National Security Council advisor for Latin American and Caribbean Affairs, explains: "When the business sector shut down Managua for the second time in a general strike in August 1978 and the middle class lined the streets to cheer the Sandinistas as they were escorted to the airport after their takeover of the National Palace, it was clear that the people of Nicaragua had had enough with forty years of Somoza rule."[12] (The people Washington counted, of course, were the business elite and middle class minority; it was they who would later be credited with making the Nicaraguan revolution, which the Sandinistas "betrayed.") The U.S. began to pressure Somoza to resign in favor of a transitional regime which would keep the National Guard and the elite intact. This strategy was branded by Nicaraguans as *Somocismo* without Somoza.

When the FSLN (Sandinista National Liberation Front) began a final offensive in May 1979, the Carter Administration attempted to intervene with a so-called "peace-keeping force" under the auspices of the Organization of American States, which would allow a new government to be set up without FSLN participation. For the first time since its founding in 1948, the OAS rejected a U.S. proposal to intervene in the Americas.[13] The U.S. continued trying, unsuccessfully, to arrange for a provisional government, first without any Sandinistas, then with a Sandinista minority. On July 17 Somoza resigned after Carter was forced to accept a Sandinista peace plan worked out with the OAS. The orderly transition plan went awry when Somoza's appointed caretaker attempted to stay in power. As the fighting continued, the National Guard disintegrated and on July 19, 1979 Sandinista fighters and supporters poured into Managua and the new Government of National Reconstruction took power.

Carter's trilateralist fallback strategy from that point on was to rely on economic aid to bolster the more conservative forces in the Reconstruction Government and help strengthen the private business sector. But the cooptation strategy never had a chance in the increasingly hardline political climate both inside and outside the Carter Administration. Carter's aid package of $75 million—targeted largely to Nicaraguan business, not the government—faced immediate opposition from conservative politicians. Congress tied the aid further to certification that Nicaragua was not "Aiding or abetting or supporting acts of violence or terrorism in other countries." Carter so certified in September 1980. But with guerrilla forces in El Salvador gaining ground, Nicaragua became the scapegoat for Carter Administration frustration with its inability to control social change in Central America.

In January 1981, just before leaving office, Carter suspended $15 million in undisbursed credits for Nicaragua, pending an investigation of Nicaragua's alleged role in supplying arms to the Salvadoran guerrillas (another $30 million still in the pipeline never reached Nicaragua) and cancelled authorization of negotiations for the renewal of Public Law 480 long-term, low-interest loans for the sale of wheat and cooking oil.[14]

## Contravention

For the Reagan Administration, it wasn't a question of how to best support so-called "moderates" in the Sandinista government, but how to overthrow that government. The 1980 Republican platform stated:

We deplore the Marxist Sandinista takeover of Nicaragua and the attempts to destabilize El Salvador, Guatemala, and Honduras...We oppose the Carter Administration aid program for the government of Nicaragua. However, we will support the efforts of the Nicaraguan people to establish a free and independent government...We will return to the fundamental principle of treating a friend as a friend and self-proclaimed enemies as enemies, without apology.

At about this time, Business International Corporation issued a forecast on Nicaragua which said the Sandinista leadership "seems to be gravitating toward a relatively moderate course"; i.e. a course which indicated a significant role for the Nicaraguan private sector and international business and banking.[15]

Nicaragua wasn't playing its assigned role of totalitarian threat. So the self-fulfilling prophecy of creating an enemy of Nicaragua went into effect. The Reagan Administration began a sophisticated disinformation campaign to win support for its as-yet unpublicized goal of overthrowing the Nicaraguan government.

The first critical phase of the disinformation campaign was the 1981 State Department "White Paper," titled "Communist Interference in El Salvador." It pretended to show a Soviet plan, based on captured documents, to arm Salvadoran rebels via Nicaragua and establish a communist base. In following months, the White Paper was thoroughly discredited in reports in the mainstream and alternative press; some documents were revealed as forgeries and genuine ones did not support U.S. charges. In June 1984, the Administration's transparent case was further damaged when David MacMichael—a CIA intelligence analyst from 1981 to 1983—charged that "the Administration and the C.I.A. have systematically misrepresented Nicaraguan involvement in the supply of arms to Salvadoran guerrillas to justify its efforts to overthrow the Nicaraguan government." There have been no verified reports of arms

# The Nicaragua Example

shipments from Nicaragua to El Salvador since April 1981.[16] But the original charge that Nicaragua is "exporting revolution" has stuck— even in the media which showed it to be false.

There has been no lack of verified reports of U.S. aid to the contras. By 1980 former national guardsmen had begun reorganizing in camps along the Honduran border with Nicaragua and in Florida. They were aided by Cuban exiles and agents of the Argentine military dictatorship then in power. By 1981 the Florida camps were receiving increased attention in the press. Although the Nicaraguans boasted of their goal of overthrowing the Sandinistas the U.S. government never took any action to enforce the Neutrality Act prohibiting private groups from making war preparations against a foreign government.

In December 1981, President Reagan signed a secret directive authorizing an initial expenditure of $19 million to conduct paramilitary operations against Nicaragua. Congressional Intelligence Committees were told that the purpose of the aid was to interdict arms allegedly being supplied by Nicaragua to the Salvadoran rebels. How anyone could believe, or even pretend to believe, such an absurd rationale is beyond me. Imagine thinking that Nicaraguan national guardsmen were willing to risk their lives as U.S. mercenaries, not to avenge their defeat and attempt to retake power, but simply to stop arms from going to a third country, El Salvador. A member of the Reagan Administration Core Group, which ran the then-secret war, told reporter Christopher Dickey that if the Intelligence Committee members didn't understand the CIA program "It was a trumped up misunderstanding." "It would

Dan Wasserman

have defied logic for anyone to think that the sole purpose of an anti-Sandinista soldier was to intercept arms traveling down a trail."[17]

As the secret war became an increasingly public one, the arms interdiction rationale was superseded by more grandiose claims: now the U.S. was supporting "freedom fighters" and countering a threat which Soviet-backed Nicaragua posed to wholesome democracies like El Salvador and to U.S. security. The disinformation campaign moved into higher gear as public opinion polls showed strong opposition to U.S. action to overthrow the Nicaraguan government and the Congress showed some sense and passed the 1982 Boland Amendment. It prohibited U.S. activity aimed at overthrowing the government of Nicaragua or provoking a military exchange between Nicaragua and Honduras.

The Reagan Administration contravened the Boland Amendment and kept on escalating the war with congressional acquiescence in practice, if not on paper. In 1983, the Reagan Administration established a Ministry of Truth called the White House Outreach Working Group on Central America. Together with the State Department's Office of Public Diplomacy it instituted a "perception management program" to better disinform the public, especially opinion makers in politics, the media, academia, business and labor.

## Pretexts

We must prevent consolidation of a Sandinista regime in Nicaragua...If we cannot prevent that, we have to anticipate the partition of Central America. Such a development would then force us to man a new military front line of the East-West conflict, right here on our continent.
UnderSecretary of Defense Fred Ikle, September 1983

The disinformation campaign embraces four basic Administration positions on Nicaragua: (1) Nicaragua is engaged in a massive military buildup serving the Soviet Union and threatening U.S. security; (2) Nicaragua's November 4, 1984 elections were a farce; (3) Nicaragua "has rejected our repeated peace efforts"; (4) The forces fighting the Nicaraguan government are "freedom fighters" committed to democracy.[18]

### Threat to U.S. Security?

Nicaragua is said to be engaged in a massive Soviet-sponsored military buildup which threatens U.S. security. This position was consolidated during the November 1984 MiG Scare, which defused concern over the CIA-contra manual and allowed the Nicaraguan elections to be more easily, wrongly dismissed as a "Soviet-style sham." The climate for congressional renewal of aid to the contras was improved and a pretext for future escalation of U.S. intervention in Nicaragua (e.g. naval quarantine, air strikes) proved its bipartisan merit. There was widespread congressional support for the Administration position that military action would be justified to destroy advanced fighter aircraft delivered to Nicaragua.

# The Nicaragua Example

As doubt grew about the MiGs' arrival Administration officials shifted attention to Nicaragua's *overall* military capability, as seen through Cold War lenses which filtered out the U.S.-backed contra war as a factor. On November 10, 1984, Secretary of State George Shultz said, "The Nicaraguans seem intent on militarizing their society and accumulating a level of weapons and armed capability that is entirely outside the standpoint of any conceivable defensive mission." Defense Department spokesman Michael Burch asserted, "We just don't feel that Nicaragua wants to be a peaceful neighbor."

In early 1980, as contra attacks were already underway, the State Department and Pentagon gave this assessment of the Nicaraguan military:

> To an even greater degree than other elements of government, the Nicaraguan defense establishment was swept away. Nothing remains except for some small arms and the battered remnants of other equipment, all of it battlescarred and most of it fit for little more than salvage. The armed forces of Nicaragua must be entirely rebuilt, both its personnel and equipment.[19]

Nicaragua's first choice for arms was the United States, but the Carter Administration responded negatively. West European countries were approached and after Francois Mitterand was elected in May 1981, France negotiated a small weapons sale to Nicaragua. The U.S. cried "stab in the back" and turned up the heat until France changed course and agreed to subject the weapons deliveries to "indefinite delays." NACLA writer Robert Mathews observes:

> France, with the world's third largest arms export industry, a popular new left-wing government and a history of relative independence from Washington proved unable to fulfill Nicaragua's hopes of Western arms supplies. For the Sandinistas, the lesson was clear. Henceforth, Nicaraguan diplomacy, trade and aid initiatives would have to factor in the Soviet bloc's exclusive role as a supplier of Nicaragua's defense needs— which escalated rapidly as Washington's preference for a military solution became ever more apparent.[20]

As Nicaragua followed the only path open in the face of a U.S. sponsored arms embargo, and turned increasingly to the Soviet Union for military assistance, the Reaganauts stepped up their charge that Nicaragua was being *built up* by the Soviets as a base for subversion of the Western hemisphere.

The Administration has published numerous reports on the alleged Soviet military buildup in Nicaragua. Like the 1981 White Paper on El Salvador they don't make their case, but they do scare people. The joint March 1985 State and Defense Department booklet, *The Soviet-Cuban Connection in Central America and the Caribbean*, devotes a whole page to grainy photos of President Daniel Ortega on official visits to the Soviet Union, East Germany and Poland (photos of Ortega's visits with Western leaders are censored). Was the Reagan-Gorbachev Smiling Summit part of a commie plot to commit subversion through photo opportunities?

Even the hardcore alleged evidence looks foolish. On page 25 of *The Soviet-Cuban Connection* there's a chart showing the Pentagon's guestimates of "Soviet-Bloc Military Deliveries to Nicaragua." Never mind the fact that it measures in tons, and you don't need many trucks, tanks or helicopters to make a lot of tons. The chart has the first jump in Soviet aid coming in 1982, two years after contra attacks began, not before then, as Reagan rhetoric has it.

Administration officials claim that Nicaragua has received more than $500 million in Soviet military aid since 1981. The most interesting point about that figure, undoubtedly inflated, is how small it is (less than the cost of five MX missiles or 16 F-15 fighters) considering that Nicaraguan armed forces had to be "entirely rebuilt" and in comparison to U.S. military aid to Central America in the same period. In FY 1985, El Salvador was authorized by Congress over $128 million in military assistance and Honduras, over $62 million, not counting assistance provided under presidential authority, supplemental assistance, reprograming and the cloak of military maneuvers. Moreover, a large part of security assistance is provided through "economic support funds," of which El Salvador was authorized $195 million in 1985.[21] According to the Caribbean Basin Information Project, the U.S. provided over $2.3 billion in security assistance to Central America between 1980 and 1984.[22]

"The most striking feature of Nicaragua's military buildup," says one analyst, "is how its rhythm has responded to specific threats and acts of aggression."[23] Some U.S. military officials have admitted to reporters that Nicaragua's Soviet weapons, including attack helicopters, surface-

## The Nicaragua Example

to-air missiles and high-speed patrol boats, are primarily defensive. If Nicaragua imported MiGs or other advanced fighters, it would improve its ability to confront contra airpower and better match its neighbors. As of early 1985, the Nicaraguan Air Force included no supersonic fighters or fighter bombers and a total of 31 less advanced fighters, trainers, transport and support craft, not including helicopters. In comparison, Honduras had 32 to 50 supersonic fighters and fighter bombers and 48 armed and unarmed trainers, transport and support craft; El Salvador had 53 supersonic fighters and fighter bombers and 64 other aircraft, not including helicopters.[24] Clearly Nicaragua cannot match U.S. airpower in or near the region. For example, the U.S. aircraft carrier, America, which has been involved in Atlantic and Caribbean maneuvers, has 85 aircraft. The idea of a Nicaragua attack on the Panama Canal, Mexico or Texas is even more absurd than the idea that the Somocistas were fighting in Nicaragua to capture guns on their way to El Salvador.

Let's entertain the loony idea that the Nicaraguans would change their current position and provide the Soviet Union with a military base (maybe like the one the U.S. has in Cuba at Guantanamo) and support the Soviets in an attack on the Panama Canal, Honduras and/or the United States. Why would the Soviet Union start World War III in such an absurd way? Nuclear missiles launched from the Soviet Union and from submarines would be far more homicidal and just as suicidal. But then, some people believe we are going to fight a drawn out *conventional* war with the Soviets. We must be sure the Nicaraguans aren't helping the Cubans attack the shipping lanes through the Panama Canal and Caribbean. We might run out of oil in a few months and have to surrender. Lucky we eliminated the threat from Grenada (population 110,000). Don't bring up embarrassing questions like, "where would Cuba and Nicaragua get their oil during this prolonged war," assuming the U.S. didn't blow them to smithereens early on. And why would the U.S. be ignoring its global war fighting plan which is premised on the notion of a prolonged, but limited *nuclear* war. It's so much simpler—and scarier—to believe the *Red Dawn* movie is for real. We'll survive World War III with the Soviets if only the Cubans and Nicaraguans aren't around to help the Russians win—provided, of course, there are enough shovels and change of address forms to go around.

The Cold War subsumes the hot war which has already killed a higher percentage of the Nicaraguan population than the U.S. lost during the Vietnam War.

Within the U.S. the war on Nicaragua has appeared as an on-again, off-again sideshow. It generates short bursts of widespread attention when Congress debates and authorizes its funding and when particularly seamy U.S. activities are exposed, such as the CIA-directed mining of Nicaragua's harbors, which set a precedent for terrorism against countries with which the U.S. has formal diplomatic relations and against international shipping. Another scandal arose over the CIA manuals providing guidance on sabotage and political assassination. Often, major events, like the bombing of Managua's international airport

Marlette

NICARAGUA ADMITTED TODAY TO THE MINING OF NEW YORK HARBOR TO FORCE THE U.S. TO CHANGE ITS GOVERNMENT TO ONE MORE ACCEPTABLE TO MANAGUA.

in 1983, are underplayed in the media and frequent contra atrocities go unreported.

For Nicaragua, the war is a constant, deadly reality. The contras have attacked private farms, peasant cooperatives, fishing boats, health clinics, hospitals, schools, childcare centers and communications, transportation and energy facilities. In October 1983, for example, the CIA supported a contra commando attack on the critical oil storage tanks at Nicaragua's only international port at Corinto; an Exxon tank was destroyed by the capitalist terrorists. Some 25,000 residents had to be evacuated; according to one of the Mexican engineers sent to help put out the fire, had more flammable products in the area been set ablaze, "not a soul would have survived." As of early 1986, over 11,000 Nicaraguans have been killed (in a population of 3 million)—almost half of them children.

The Reagan Administration provided some $140 million to the contras between 1981 and 1985. When Congress temporarily cut off funds in October 1984, contra aid didn't dry up. The Administration directed contra operations from the National Security Council and funneled additional assistance through Honduras, El Salvador, Taiwan, South Korea and Israel. Moreover, it has encouraged private, rightwing groups such as the U.S. Council for World Freedom—affiliated with the World Anti-Communist League, a coalition of conservative and fascist groups founded in 1967[25]—to provide funds to the contras and arranged military transportation for so-called "humanitarian" donations. Meanwhile, the Pentagon has used a continual series of military exercises in Honduras to channel unauthorized supplies and equipment to the contras and construct airfields, radar sites, roads, fuel depots and other facilities in a relentless buildup of U.S. forces in the region.

# The Nicaragua Example

The U.S. has conducted major naval maneuvers off the Atlantic and Pacific Coasts of Nicaragua, guided the mining of Nicaraguan harbors and supplied contras with aircraft used in supply runs and bombing attacks. Electronic surveillance ships keep a constant watch and surveillance planes repeatedly violate Nicaraguan airspace; at the time of the MiGs crisis, they made a point of creating sonic booms over Managua.

The MiGs scare boosted the case of officials inside the Administration who want to more quickly intensify pressure on Nicaragua. As reported by Philip Taubman in the *New York Times*, one official said, "Some of those who want us to adopt a harder line have long wished that MiGs would be delivered because they know that would tilt the policy in their direction."

## Electoral Farce?

Since the Administration describes itself as supporting the "democratic resistance" in Nicaragua, it could not ascribe any legitimacy to the Nicaraguan elections of November 4, 1984 without contradicting its own position. It follows that if the Administration is to continue to destabilize the Nicaraguan government, it must treat the elections as a sham, whatever their true nature, and insist that it supports "free elections." In Reagan's words, "we stood for democracy in the Philippines." "We have to stand for democracy in Nicaragua."

The U.S. has a long-held double-standard around democratic elections: it has supported rightwing dictatorships which "legitimize" their rule with fraudulent elections as Somoza did and destabilized democratically-elected governments which were not to U.S. liking, such as the Arbenz government in Guatemala, 1954, and the Allende government in Chile, 1973. In a 1970 meeting to discuss measures to prevent Salvador Allende from winning the presidential election, Henry Kissinger declared, "I don't see why we need to stand by and watch a country go Communist due to the irresponsibility of its own people."[26]

According to former *New York Times* senior editor John Oakes, "The most fraudulent thing about the Nicaraguan election was the part the Reagan Administration played in it. By their own admission, United States Embassy officials in Managua pressured opposition politicians to withdraw from the ballot in order to isolate the Sandinistas and to discredit the regime."[27] Some two weeks before the election, the *New York Times* reported this acknowledgement from a Reagan official:

> The Administration never contemplated letting [Arturo] Cruz stay in the race, because then the Sandinistas could justifiably claim that the elections were legitimate, making it much harder for the United States to oppose the Nicaraguan government.[28]

The U.S. media played its required part and followed the Administration lead in reporting on the election, particularly in using the candidacy of Arturo Cruz as a litmus test of legitimacy—negating its own reporting to the contrary. In fact, Cruz represented a rightwing coalition which had no chance of winning a fair election.[29] Cruz, who broke with the revolutionary government after serving as ambassador to the U.S., represented the Democratic Coordinating Committee (CDN or Coordinadora), an alliance of the Superior Council of Private Enterprise (COSEP) and the four most conservative political parties: Constitutionalist Liberal Party, PLC, with barely a few hundred members; Social Democratic Party, PSD, the vehicle of *La Prensa* editor Pedro Joaquin Chamorro (now in self-imposed exile); Social Christian Party, PSC, the largest and least conservative member of the coalition; and the Nicaraguan Conservative Party, PCN, founded in June 1984. COSEP has received $150,000 from the U.S. Endowment for Democracy, and *La Prensa*—which was a partisan of the CDN during the election, and not the voice of an "independent" press or even of the other opposition—has received $100,000. According to the report of the U.S. Latin American Studies Association (LASA) Delegation, "The weight of the evidence [including CDN sources] suggests that the Coordinadora group made a policy decision to pursue its political goals in 1984 outside of the electoral process; and there is circumstantial evidence, reinforced by a senior U.S. diplomat in Central America with whom the group talked, that the decision not to run was made as early as December 1983."[30]

According to the LASA report, "The electoral process was designed, through months of debate in the Council of State [and consultation with West European countries], to create the greatest possibility for minority party representation, using a standard model of proportional representation. This model tilts the system toward much more pluralism than would have been created, for example, by a U.S.-style single-member district system...Both the registration process and the voting process was designed meticulously to minimize the potential for abuses. The Nicaraguans used Swedish technical assistance in the design of the registration cards, ballots, the precinct procedures, and the reporting procedures." All parties in the election were given equal allotments of free air time on television.

Over 1.1 million Nicaraguans voted, representing a high turnout of 75.4 percent of the registered electorate (93.7 percent of the estimated voting-age population was registered during national registration days). FSLN presidential candidate, Daniel Ortega, won with 67 percent of the vote and the FSLN won 61 of 96 seats in the National Assembly. The Democratic Conservative Party (PCD) came in second, winning 14 percent of the presidential vote and 14 Assembly seats. The Independent Liberal Party (PLI) was considered the strongest opposition to the FSLN, but less than two weeks before the election their presidential candidate, Virgilio Godoy, announced he and the party were withdrawing; the vice-presidential candidate and several Assembly candidates continued running and in this confused situation the PLI ended up with 9.6 percent of the vote and 9 seats. The Popular Social Christian Party (PPSC) won 5.6 percent and 6 seats, and three leftwing parties—the Socialist Party (PSN), Communist Party (PCdeN) and Marxist-Leninist Popular Action Movement (MAP-ML)—split 3.8 percent of the vote and won 2 seats each.

# The Nicaragua Example

Most international observers, including LASA, the mission sent by the Washington Office on Latin America and the International Human Rights Law Group and the British Parliamentary Human Rights Group, judged the elections to be free—whatever specific shortcomings they cited.

**Rejecting Peace Efforts?**
In the words of President Reagan's April 1983 speech to Congress, Nicaragua "has rejected our repeated peace efforts." Once again, Reagan has rejected reality. As early as February 1981, when the U.S. released the White Paper, Nicaragua called for joint Nicaraguan-Honduran border patrols. The U.S. preferred joint U.S.-Honduran military maneuvers. In October 1981, Nicaragua endorsed the now-forgotten French-Mexican proposal for a negotiated settlement in El Salvador. The U.S. wanted a military victory in both El Salvador and Nicaragua. In November, Reagan authorized the first official installment of contra assistance.

Roy Gutman, a defense and foreign affairs reporter for *Newsday*, describes the U.S. role in negotiations with Nicaragua as "America's Diplomatic Charade":

"What's wrong with a little target practice?"

Roger

From late 1981 until summer 1984, when Secretary of State George Shultz visited Managua, the exchanges seemed to be mainly posturing for public effect. Indeed, at no point were U.S. demands, which have changed at a dizzying pace, formally presented in writing. Although the Sandinistas bear some of the blame for the failure of diplomacy, throughout the on-again, off-again talks U.S. officials operated in a manner that guaranteed their failure. After the August 1981 talks broke down, the administration's energies went into a build-up of military pressure...American rhetoric became increasingly shrill and by late 1983 progress toward already-stated U.S. goals [e.g. curtailing Nicaraguan aid for the Salvadoran FMLN] no longer was the criterion for success.[31]

The "diplomatic charade" only got worse. When progress was made in the Contadora negotiations during December and January 1983-84, the Reagan Administration responded with the mining of Nicaragua's harbors. In September 1984, a Contadora draft treaty was endorsed by the four sponsoring nations—Mexico, Venezuela, Colombia and Panama—after 20 months of negotiations with Nicaragua, Honduras, El Salvador, Costa Rica and Guatemala. It contained provisions for the withdrawal of foreign military advisers, prohibition of foreign military bases and interference in the internal affairs of other countries and controls on the level of arms and troops in the region, and it calls for the establishment of conditions for free elections. By most accounts, Nicaragua surprised the Reagan Administration by signing the treaty on September 21 (although Nicaragua had also signed an earlier draft in January 1984). The Administration responded by persuading its allies in the region to make new objections to the treaty, calling it unverifiable and favorable to Nicaragua. A secret National Security Council paper takes pride in the successful U.S. sabotage of the Contadora Treaty: "We have trumped the latest Nicaraguan/Mexican efforts to rush signature of an unsatisfactory Contadora agreement."

Washington's problem with the September 1984 Contadora draft treaty is that it is symmetrical and not biased in favor of the U.S.; i.e. it would eliminate U.S. military maneuvers in the region and prohibit U.S. military bases and advisers, not just Cuban and Soviet, and it would require suspension of outside aid to the contras as well as the FMLN (which is far less dependent upon outside assistance in obtaining military supplies; much FMLN weaponry is captured from the Salvadoran Army or bought from Salvadoran soldiers). A September 1985 draft treaty favors the U.S. by calling, for example, only for a reduction in international military maneuvers with "a view to their elimination." Because the U.S. employs these maneuvers to supply the contras and strengthen U.S. forces in the region, the Nicaraguan government rejects this formulation, as well as other changes in the draft favoring the United States.[32]

On January 18, 1985, the Administration suspended the bilateral negotiations with Nicaragua which had been taking place since June 1984 in Manzanillo, Mexico. Also on January 18, the Reagan Administration walked out on proceedings in the International Court of Justice (World Court) over Nicaragua's suit against the United States. In May 1984, the World Court had issued a preliminary ruling that the U.S.

# The Nicaragua Example

should immediately halt any attempts to mine or blockade Nicaraguan ports and said that Nicaragua's political independence "should be fully respected and should not be jeopardized by any military or paramilitary activities."

On November 26, the Court ruled in a 15-1 decision that it had jurisdiction to rule on Nicaragua's suit charging the U.S. with illegally supporting paramilitary activities and urging the Court to order the U.S. to stop the attacks and pay reparations. Reagan officials argue that the Court is erroneous in its judgement in the case and imply that it is becoming politicized against the interests of the West. However, according to international law expert Richard Falk, "Nicaragua went to the World Court to argue its case against the United States within a judicial framework generally regarded as unsympathetic to Third World positions on international issues." The U.S. has received numerous favorable rulings on other World Court cases, such as the U.S. suit against Iran over the seizure of American diplomats; Iran refused to take part in the proceedings and the Court went on to rule that the Iranian actions were illegal. This time it is the United States which is refusing to submit to international law.

On December 2, 1985 Secretary of State Shultz asserted that the U.S. had no intention of resuming direct negotiations with Nicaragua. Earlier reports in the press indicated that there was no chance of a negotiated settlement with a Sandinista-led government.[33] The U.S. continues to sabotage the Contadora process, now rejuvenated with the support of Brazil, Argentina, Peru and Uruguay, and with the January 1986 Declaration of Carabelleda endorsed by Nicaragua, El Salvador,

Honduras, Guatemala and Costa Rica. Congressman Barnes has described Reagan policy this way: "a negotiated settlement with the Sandinista regime is possible only if it ceases to be the Sandinista regime; and the only thing to be negotiated in El Salvador is the terms of the left's surrender. In short, U.S. policy leaves no room for settlements at all."[34] Perhaps he will remember that as Congress debates whether to give the Administration new funding for the contras. Fresh from the Philippines, Ambassador Philip Habib leads the next round of the diplomacy charade, intended, as always, to buy time and resources for military action.

**Freedom Fighters?**
President Reagan has called the contras "our brothers," the "moral equal of our founding fathers." In testimony before Congress in January 1985, then Assistant Secretary of State for InterAmerican Affairs Langhorne Motley claimed: "The freedom fighters are peasants, farmers, shopkeepers, and vendors. Their leaders are without exception men who opposed Somoza."

Motley's lie was a big one. Former Somoza guard officers dominate the military hierarchy of the FDN, the central contra force. In a staff report, the Congressional Arms Control and Foreign Policy Caucus found that 46 of the 48 positions in the FDN's military command structure are held by former guardsmen.[35]

The CIA has tried to graft a figurehead non-Somocista political leadership on the Somocista military leaders. In December 1982 the CIA created a six-member "political directorate." Edgar Chamorro, chief public spokesman for the directorate until he was forced out in November 1984, describes the CIA briefing and rehearsal which preceded the press conference announcing the new directorate:

> [CIA agent Tony] Feldman introduced two lawyers from Washington who briefed us on the Neutrality Act, the American law prohibiting private citizens from waging war on another country from U.S. territory. Feldman was worried we were going to tell the press that we were trying to overthrow the Sandinistas, which, of course, is exactly what we wanted to do. He emphasized that we should say instead that we were trying to "create conditions for democracy." After the briefing we asked each other the questions we were likely to face in the morning...
> "Have you had any contact with U.S. government officials?"
> The CIA men agreed there was no way to finesse this one. We simply had to lie and say, "No."[36]

Adolfo Calero was selected by the CIA to be "president" of the directorate. In his affidavit to the World Court case on Nicaragua, Edgar Chamorro explains: "Calero had been working for the C.I.A. in Nicaragua for a long time. He served as, among other things, a conduit of funds from the United States Embassy to various student and labor organizations. 'Feldman' had told me that the C.I.A. was bringing him out of Nicaragua, where he had run the local Coca-Cola distributorship," to serve on the directorate.[37]

Writing in a *New York Times* op-ed on June 24, 1985, Chamorro asserted:

# The Nicaragua Example

My experience as a former rebel leader convinced me that the Nicaraguan Democratic Force cannot contribute to the democratization of Nicaragua. The rebels are in the hands of former National Guardsmen who control the contra army, stifle internal dissent and intimidate or murder those who oppose them.

Before he was groomed by the Reagan Administration as the Jose Napoleon Duarte of Nicaragua—the Saint Moderate who would tame the extremists of right and left—Arturo Cruz seemed to share Chamorro's opinion of contra character. In a summer 1983 *Foreign Affairs* article, Cruz wrote of support for the former Somoza guardsmen:

> Carrying perhaps an even greater responsibility, those who sustain the forces inimical to the Sandinistas must not ignore the fact that idealistic young boys and girls constitute the Revolution's rank and file. Therefore, those who aid insurrection in my country—whose disenchantment with the Revolution's course and concern for the security of their own country I do not dispute—should be aware of the risk they take of bearing a historical responsibility for contributing, albeit indirectly and unintentionally, to a possible mass execution of the flower of our youth.[38]

"Frankly, I think he's had a bum rap!"

Paul Conrad

Today Cruz is a leader of the UNO (Unified Nicaraguan Opposition) along with Adolfo Calero and Alfonso Robelo, co-founder of ARDE with Eden Pastora. But reports indicate he is growing frustrated with his lack of real influence within the UNO.[39]

In *Contra Terror in Nicaragua*, Reed Brody documents how contra forces have committed repeated assaults upon the Nicaraguan people, including rape, kidnapping, torture, mutilation, murder and massacres. In account after gruesome account, he describes contra atrocities, including decapitation, using women and children for target practice, gang rape and other forms of torture and mutilation, including castration, gouging out eyes and cutting out tongues, ears and noses. Nicaraguans call the contras *bestia*, beast.

The U.S. bears direct responsibility for contra atrocities. The contras are a U.S. proxy army. In March 1984, an unnamed "U.S. diplomat in Honduras" described the contra role as a no-lose "instrument of pressure":

> The contras are strictly an instrument of pressure. Some people around here and in Washington really thought—and still do, I guess—that they could incite an insurrection and overthrow the Sandinistas. I always thought that was a lot of crap. But in any event, the theory was that we couldn't lose. If they took Managua, wonderful. If not, the idea was that the Sandinistas would react one of two ways. Either they'd liberalize and stop exporting revolution, which is fine and dandy, *or they'd tighten up, alienate their own people, their international support and their backers in the United States, in the long run making themselves much more vulnerable. In a way, that one was even better*—or so the idea went.[40] (Emphasis added.)

## Knocking Down the Walls

On a visit to Nicaragua in 1984, I had the opportunity to meet with Dora Maria Tellez as part of a delegation sponsored by MADRE, a U.S.-Central American friendship association. Dora Maria Tellez, now Minister of Health, was a Sandinista guerrilla leader and has held various party and government posts since 1979. We asked her how she compared the revolutionary struggle with running the government. She answered:

> An absolute difference. If they give you the work of knocking down this house, you start breaking walls, windows, everything. But if they tell you now build the house, first you have to learn to be a stonemason, then learn the ratio of cement to stone, dig up the old foundation, put in the new foundation, put up the walls. And when you've put the walls up, the roof on, everything else, then you have to fix the inside of the house—furniture and so on.

When asked about Reagan's impact, Tellez responded:

> What would we do if there was no Reagan? We destroyed the house, dug out the foundation, put in a new foundation and started putting up the house. When we're putting up a wall, Reagan comes and knocks down one we've put up on the other side. So, we have to rebuild the wall he knocked over, and while we're doing that, he knocks over a different one. If he weren't there we could finish the house, and even put the roof on!

Not only does the U.S. keep knocking down walls, it blames Nicaragua for being an inept builder. Just as the Nicaraguan military buildup is discussed without reference to the war, so too are the country's economic problems. Yet, common sense would indicate that wartime destruction, rising defense costs, economic embargo and an effective, but little publicized, U.S. campaign to block international credit and assistance would promote economic problems. Indeed, that's exactly what the U.S. intends. All of this comes on top of the billions of dollars in damage and capital flight during the insurrection against Somoza, and in the context of economic crisis throughout Latin America.

Contrary to the "doom and gloom" which passes for Administration information on Sandinista economic policies, Nicaragua had the highest rate of economic growth and investment in Latin America between 1980 and 1983 (according to the U.N. Economic Commission for Latin America). In 1983, Nicaragua's gross national product grew by 5.1 percent while other Latin American economies declined. The agrarian reform program has been highly successful; crop production rose 38.6 percent between 1981 and 1983. Between 1979 and 1983, the government undertook extensive rural electrification and water purification projects and greatly expanded health, education, daycare and other social services. Illiteracy was reduced from 52 to 12 percent; infant mortality was halved, to the lowest level in Central America; polio and measles were virtually eradicated and, in 1982, Nicaragua received a World Health Organization award for the greatest achievement in health by a Third World nation.[41]

Contra attacks have wreaked havoc on Nicaragua's ability to maintain and expand reconstruction achievements since the revolution. Nicaragua now devotes some 50 percent of the national budget to the war effort. Health workers, teachers and government employees in agriculture, construction and other ministries have been special contra targets—with U.S. knowledge. Duane "Dewey" Clarridge, former CIA division chief in charge of Nicaraguan paramilitary operations, told congressional committees in a secret briefing in late 1983 that "civilians and Sandinista officials in the provinces, as well as heads of cooperatives, nurses, doctors and judges" had been killed by the contras. He explained that this didn't contradict the presidential directive against assassination because "These events don't constitute assassinations because as far as we are concerned assassinations are only those of heads of state."[42]

When the Reagan Administration declared an embargo in May 1985—describing Nicaragua as "an unusual and extraordinary threat to the national security and foreign policy of the United States"—it was one more step in a systematic campaign designed to isolate and destabilize Nicaragua. Reagan is not being contradictory as some critics allege, pushing Nicaragua into the hands of the Soviet Union. Washington is quite purposefully creating a self-fulfilling prophecy: insuring that Nicaragua moves closer to Washington's portrait of Soviet proxy, thereby strengthening the contra lobby in the United States. Daniel Ortega's trip to Moscow—ill-timed for U.S. politics, but quite legitimate

## Corporate Camelot: Guatemala

ED RABEL, CBS Reporter: Americans have fought for a long time to stay in Guatemala. There was also a lot to be had. One big American company had almost all of it. The whole country of Guatemala was once virtually a branch office of the United Fruit Company. In the 1950's, it held two-thirds of the usable farm land and monopolized the nation's railroad in its multi-million-dollar banana empire. When a democratically-elected president named Jacobo Arbenz tried to institute a land reform program in 1954 so that poor farmers could have land of their own, United Fruit lobbied the Eisenhower Administration to intervene. The CIA stepped in and overthrew the Guatemalan leader...From that day to this, Guatemalans have lived under nearly constant Government harassment...

[Rabel interviewed Fred Sherwood, former head of the U.S. Chamber of Commerce in Guatemala]

Sherwood's own personal holdings are considerable: a rubber plantation, a cement factory, and part of a textile mill which he manages. It's an ideal place to invest, he says, because profits are high, costs are low. Sherwood pays workers at his textile mill about four dollars and fifty cents a day...

RABEL: Is the government pretty cooperative?

SHERWOOD: Oh, yes. They're very cooperative. We don't have restrictions as to environmental things and there's just no restrictions or rules at all, so that makes it nice.

RABEL: Are the people here oppressed in any way?

SHERWOOD: Really, I don't think so. I know of no individual, I know of no one—I have lived here for 36 years, I've been in farming, in industry, in commerce—and I don't know of anybody being impressed [sic]. No one forces them to do anything. And I think this is just something that some reporters have thought up.

RABEL: ...I want to ask you a question about something a [Christian Democrat] politician here in this country told me. And he said that more than 120 of his party's leaders had been assassinated in about an 18-month period. I'm just wondering what you make of—of that kind of statement.

SHERWOOD: Well, first place, I'd very much question it, because I don't think there's been a hundred and twenty people of all types assassinated here in the—in the last year. I mean, I'm not counting the peasants or the—I mean men of that category. No, I think that's probably exaggerated to a great extent. There were a couple of politicians assassinated a couple of years ago, but believe me, they were way out in left field and well, these people are, I think, our enemies. They're—they're against our—our way of life. And maybe assassination is not the right word for it, but I don't think they should be—continue allowed to run free to try to destroy our form of government, our way of life, in other words.

Source: Transcript of "Guatemala," CBS Reports, with CBS News correspondent Ed Rabel, broadcast September 1, 1982.

# The Nicaragua Example

from the Nicaraguan perspective—became the excuse eagerly grabbed by many Democrats to relieve themselves of the burden of opposition. U.S. politicians consider it an insult when Nicaragua acts like a sovereign country, and not a neocolony.

The real threat to U.S. elites is the "threat of a good example." That Nicaragua will succeed in pursuing a non-aligned path outside the U.S. bloc and the Soviet bloc. That it will succeed in building a working mixed economy of private and public enterprise. That it will succeed in creating a pluralistic, participatory democratic political system. That it will succeed in raising living standards. That it will succeed in agrarian reform, achieving food self-sufficiency and wiping out malnutrition. That it will succeed in achieving a high degree of literacy and education. That it will succeed in achieving equal rights and participation for women.

The threat of this success to the U.S. is not the "loss" of Nicaragua itself as a cheap labor and resource provider. Direct U.S. corporate investment in Nicaragua was never very high, although it had great impact upon Nicaragua (70 major U.S. corporations operated in Nicaragua in 1979 compared with 300 U.S.-controlled firms in Guatemala), and many investors pursued good relations with the new government. It is the cumulative "loss" of Central America, the Caribbean and South America as a captive sphere that so threatens the U.S. The threat is not that the Soviet Union will gain the region. It won't. The threat is that the U.S. will lose its hegemony.

Nicaraguans are not fighting for the Soviet Union, but for their own lives, livelihoods and self-determination. Today, the "average U.S. cat eats more beef than the average Central American person."[43] Some 50,000 Nicaraguans died in the rebellion against *Somocismo* and its hunger, illiteracy and terror. It is not the destiny of Central Americans to be miserable, as Jeane Kirkpatrick preaches. It is the legacy of colonialism and neocolonialism. It is the legacy of the U.S. "right" to intervene. It is a legacy that must end.

# BEYOND ARROGANCE AND PARANOIA

Across the "relevant" spectrum, there is a shared belief in the right to intervene. In June 1985, as Congress debated whether to supply so-called "humanitarian aid" to the contras, House majority leader Jim Wright warned that approval would mean, "For the first time we're going to be saying that we are accessories to overthrowing the government of Nicaragua." Both the House and Senate gave Reagan a green light for further intervention under the transparent guise of "humanitarian aid."

Dissenting Democrats only go so far in their opposition, lest they risk being blamed for "losing" Central America to the "communists." When rollbackers demand that they choose between supporting Reagan and the contras or "Ortega and the communists," the Democrats scream briefly about McCarthyite tactics, and then scurry into the cloakrooms to save the Reagan Doctrine from its rhetoric with war by compromise.

When the liberal interventionists attempt to stand and debate, they generally totter, with one foot underneath and the other skidding toward the right. They conduct their discussion in an East-West framework even as they claim to understand indigenous events. Congressman Barnes writes: "Fidel Castro did not plant this garden; he is just shaking the trees and waiting for the ripe fruit to fall into his hands."[1] The liberals argue that the way to prevent "another Cuba" in Nicaragua, or "another Nicaragua" in El Salvador is to reform and negotiate. The right responds, falsely but persuasively, you were hoodwinked by the Sandinistas before, and you'll be hoodwinked again. Commies can't be trusted. Conceding most of the ground to the right when it comes to fundamental assumptions, the liberals look naive and foolish. Witness neoliberal Congressman Stephen Solarz arguing the reformist case for the Philippines, in a February 16, 1986 *New York Times* op-ed, genuflecting to the right on Nicaragua and the "communist threat":

A Communist victory would, indeed, be a political disaster for the Philippines and a strategic debacle for us. But what [some in the Reagan Administration] fail to appreciate is that Mr. Marcos is the No. 1 recruiting agent for the Communist Party in the Philippines. The longer he remains in power the greater the chances that the Communists will prevail. Those who fear the consequences of Mr. Marcos's resignation or removal look to what happened in Iran and Nicaragua after the fall of the Shah and the Somoza dynasty. They conclude that, while Mr. Marcos may not exactly be a choir boy, he is "our son of a bitch," as Franklin Delano Roosevelt once said of Anastasio Somoza. Most Americans agree that the mullahs and *the Sandinistas are far worse than the tyrants they replaced*. It does not necessarily follow, however, that the demise of an authoritarian government inevitably leads to an even more repressive regime. [Emphasis added.]

The Sandinistas, in reality, are infinitely better than the tyrant they replaced. But that is not the real concern of U.S. policymakers. The real concern is that the Sandinistas dare to be sovereign. In his commentary following Corazon Aquino's ascendancy in the Philippines, CBS News anchor Dan Rather expressed concern that the Filipinos might move toward a "non-aligned" "Third Worldist" policy. Stripped of the camouflage red of communism, the "threat" is self-determination.

A utopian view of U.S. foreign policy has gained currency in the wake of the fall of Marcos in the Philippines and Duvalier in Haiti. In the words of *New York Times* commentator Anthony Lewis, "There is a new consensus in this country on human rights in foreign policy. Americans across the political spectrum are not prepared to tolerate crude abuses of power by tyrants simply because they call themselves 'pro-American.' "[2]

There is no such consensus. U.S. foreign policy has always rested upon the abuse of power by itself and its allies, and it does so today. It will do so until the U.S. is prepared to drop its special claim to the labor and resources of other countries. Liberals are not prepared to drop this claim, for upon it rests the privileges of the U.S. ruling class of which they are a part. What liberals are prepared to do differently than the right, is negotiate the terms upon which this claim is enforced.

## The Democracy Doctrine: A Trojan Horse

What happened in the Philippines was not an American celebration of global democracy, but a demonstration election gone awry. As authors Frank Brodhead and Edward Herman argue, a demonstration election is designed to legitimize a U.S.-backed regime in the eyes of the American public.[3] In the hollow center of this Trojan Horse democracy are the weapons of counterinsurgency.

Reagan officials did not expect the opposition to unite around Cory Aquino and Doy Laurel. They expected Marcos to win reelection as he did in 1981, when George Bush toasted him, "We love your adherence to the democratic principle and democratic process." They expected Marcos's electoral fix to work, not backfire. When it became clear that the groundswell of support behind Aquino would drown Marcos, no matter how hard he tried to steal the election, Reagan officials apparently tried for a next-best demonstration election: a partial fraud through which

Marcos would allow Aquino's more conservative vice presidential candidate Laurel to win and join a transitional coalition government. In one of the more obscene displays of electoral intervention by the U.S. media, *Nightline* host Ted Koppel pressed Laurel to commit himself to accept the vice presidency under Marcos in order to "heal the wounds" of Filipino society.

Special Ambassador Philip Habib apparently went to Manila to arrange a coalition government; whether with or without Aquino is not clear. Aquino had the mettle to hold out for victory, and the U.S. found again that dictators don't go quietly just because Washington finds they have outlived their usefulness. Marcos would leave only after the U.S.-sanctioned military rebellion by Defense Minister Enrile and General Ramos, two key bridges between the Marcos past and the Aquino future.

Just as Duarte's democratic credentials opened the floodgates to U.S. support for counterinsurgency in El Salvador, so it is hoped that Aquino and the refurbished military will be able to wage a victorious campaign against the revolutionary New People's Army. At this writing, one can only hope that Aquino will attempt to follow up her unexpectedly broad release of political prisoners and pursue serious peace negotiations with the rebels as part of a genuine commitment to radical transformation of the Philippine political economy. Whatever Aquino's actual motives, however, the U.S. will apply intense pressure for a rebel defeat and minimal reform.

These have been busy times for U.S. proconsuls. News reports indicate that the U.S. ambassador to Haiti, Clayton McManaway Jr.—a CIA veteran heavily involved in the Phoenix program death squads in Vietnam, which, according to the former CIA station chief in Saigon, William Colby, achieved the "neutralization" of nearly 60,000 Vietnamese—"played a role in deciding the composition of the military-dominated government" in talks which "reportedly began at least a week before Mr. Duvalier fled on February 7 to France."[4]

U.S. policyshapers across the "relevant" spectrum are clearly enamored with their growing role in bringing "democracy" to the neocolonies. The Democracy Doctrine is a bipartisan show. The media loves it.

The Philippines gave us "The Smiling Revolution." Expect a future mini-series: "South Korea: Saga of the Two Kims." In early March a delegation of U.S. politicians went to South Korea to "assess chances for greater democracy." At a news conference at the home of opposition leader Kim Dae Jung, Representative Thomas Foglietta of Pennsylvania remarked, "We are not trying to force our ways of life to [sic] South Koreans. But we want to export the finest American product—democracy."[5]

What country will be next? Chile without Pinochet? What about Paraguay, Zaire, Saudi Arabia? Imagine a "Lifestyles of the Rich and Tyrannical" report from the homes of the Saudi dynasty.

Countries are made safe for U.S.-style democracy through terror. Two political parties are preferred: the dictator's party and the "mode-

# Beyond Arrogance and Paranoia

rate" (i.e. pro-U.S.) opposition. Death squads "disappear" large numbers of reformers and radicals, and frighten the "moderates." Surviving popular radical leaders are best kept in exile or jail until the election is over, as in Uruguay. If Nicaragua had followed the U.S. example, it would have eliminated all opposition forces and then held an election.

The Democracy Doctrine is a response to popular revolt. It aims to preserve the authoritarian global rule of the United States. In the Philippines the perceived stakes are the Subic Bay and Clark Air bases, with their nearby prostitution enclaves, and multinational corporate investment, especially in the export processing zones (free trade zones), where wages for U.S.-owned electronic plants are $34 to $46 a month.[6]

The Democracy Doctrine won't work in the long run. People can't eat ballots. Just as the "Alliance for Progress" left a string of national security states in its wake—demolishing established democracies in Brazil, Uruguay, Chile and elsewhere—so the Democracy Doctrine may lead to the same result as the needs of the poor majorities press against the barricades of elite U.S. interests.

The debt crisis will play an important role. In 1984 Third World governments owed Western governments and banks $895 billion—a sum equivalent to the money poured into armaments around the world. The seven largest debtor countries are Brazil, Mexico, Argentina, Venezuela, South Korea, the Philippines and Indonesia.[7] Much of the money has been poured down the ratholes of corrupt regimes which welcomed Western corporations in the mutually-beneficial plunder of their countries.

Peasants and workers are being told to accept deadly austerity in order to pay the debts of their current or former oppressors. But when you are malnourished, "belt tightening" means starvation. People don't voluntarily commit themselves and their children to hunger.

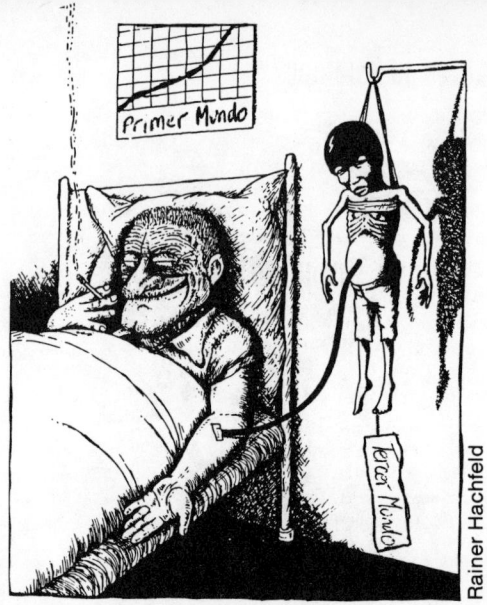

## Perpetual Siege

During a visit by a group of U.S. citizens with a U.S. Ambassador in Central America who has since been transferred, the Ambassador was asked to explain how such U.S. actions as the mining of Nicaragua's harbors and bombing of airports differed from the acts of terrorism that the U.S. condemned around the world. The reply, off the record, was, "Well, you're not going to like this answer, but if they do it it's terrorism, if we do it, it's fighting for freedom."[8]

The U.S. is the world's greatest terrorist state and few Americans know it. Directly and indirectly, the U.S. has placed much of the world under perpetual siege. The siege of the national security state. Or the siege of so-called low-intensity conflict. Blood runs, but it is mainly Third World blood. It flows outside the everyday eyes of the mainstream media. It doesn't really count.

El Salvador is a good example of terrorism under the Democracy Doctrine. In *The Continuing Terror*, Americas Watch reports that "President Duarte's civilian government notwithstanding, the human rights situation in El Salvador remains terrible." Violations include: "aerial bombardments, strafing, mortaring and Army ground operations that kill, maim and terrorize the civilian population and that deprive them of the food they need to survive"; "a resurgence in death squad activity"; and the "continuing, selective use of torture by the security forces, including such methods as electronic shock, hangings by arms and legs, the *capucha* (a hood that makes breathing impossible) and beatings."[9]

The United States bears direct responsibility for this terrible human rights situation. According to Allan Nairn:

Early in the 1960s, during the Kennedy Administration, agents of the U.S. government in El Salvador set up two official security organizations that killed thousands of peasants and suspected leftists over the next fifteen years. These organizations, guided by American operatives, developed into the paramilitary apparatus that came to be known as the Salvadoran Death Squads.

Today, even as the Reagan Administration publicly condemns the Death Squads, the CIA—in violation of U.S. law—continues to provide training, support, and intelligence to security forces directly involved in Death Squad activity.[10]

U.S. arrogance and paranoia come to bear nicely in concentrating attention upon so-called "international terrorism." International terrorism means acts of violence directed against Americans, rather than practiced by Americans. There is no comparison in the scope and intensity of violence. As Ed Herman points out in his book, *The Real Terror Network*:

At the First Latin American Congress of Relatives of the Disappeared, held in San Jose, Costa Rica, January 20-24, 1981, the estimate given for disappeared men, women and children in Latin America over the past two decades was 90,000. By contrast, the CIA's most recent (newly inflated) estimate of the total number of deaths resulting from "international terrorist" violence for the period 1968-1980, numbers 3,668, or about 4 percent of the number of "disappearances" for Latin America alone.[11]

Since then, the numbers of disappeared have risen—many at the hands of death squads in El Salvador and Guatemala. These disappearers weren't trained in Libya or the Soviet Union, but rather at the U.S. Army School of the Americas in Panama, the Special Warfare Center in Fort Bragg, North Carolina, and local police and military headquarters.

"International terrorism" transforms the most mellow liberals into Rambo cheerleaders, shifting the debate over foreign policy even further to the right. Following the attack on the Rome airport, Senator Howard Metzenbaum fixed the blame on Libya and asserted in a television interview, "Maybe we're at that point in the world where Mr. Khadafy has to be eliminated." He added that he intended his remark to be taken literally, meaning assassination.[12]

There is racism, of course, in all of this. Violence against Third World people is "freedom fighting" or "low-intensity conflict" or, at worst, the renegade actions of unrepentant rightwing "extremists." Terrorism is violence by Arabs and other people of color against white people. When Palestinian Alex Odeh, the West Coast director of the American Arab Anti-Discrimination League, was assassinated in the U.S. it was only briefly reported and largely forgotten. The *New York Times* didn't run front page spreads with his picture. The networks didn't hound his family and friends for reaction stories. That would spoil the international terrorist plot, so useful in distracting attention from the perpetual siege.

## It's Mourning Again in America

The American National Insecurity State is busily defending global interests it has no right to claim, and becoming more xenophobic as the rightful claimants rebel.

Military spending is heading skyward. Fiscal Year 1986 defense outlays "will be the highest (in constant dollars) since 1946 except for peak spending for the Korean and Vietnam wars."[13] The costs of U.S. militarism can best be described in comparisons:

\*The 1981-85 U.S. military budget of over $2 trillion greatly exceeded the sum total of "a year's worth of all the goods and services—the combined gross national products—of Latin America, Australia, Africa, Southeast Asia, and India, plus all the oil produced in the Middle East."[14]

\* "The budget of the US Air Force is larger than the total educational budget for 1.2 billion children in Africa, Latin America, and Asia excluding Japan."

\* "It costs $590,000 a day to operate one aircraft carrier and every day in Africa alone 14,000 children die of hunger or hunger-related causes."[15]

According to Ruth Sivard's *World Military and Social Expenditures*, there are enough nuclear weapons to kill every person now living 12 times over. Meanwhile, "one adult in three cannot read and write, one person in four is hungry."[16]

Behind the "new patriotism," with its chant of "USA, Number One!" there is a new impoverishment. One out of six Americans lives below the poverty line; that includes one out of every four children under six years of age, and one out of every two Black children.[17] Two out of three poor adults are women. In this, the richest country in the world, there are nearly 40 million poor—a sum greater than the combined populations of Canada, Honduras, Nicaragua and El Salvador.

Downward mobility is the new norm. Bonafide yuppies are rare. "Today, a 30-year-old male head of household earns about 10 percent less in real buying power than his father did at the same age."[18] What was once recession-level unemployment is now called recovery. The new floor for unemployment is about 7 percent, not counting millions too discouraged to keep looking for work and working part-time jobs because they can't find more. Over 40 percent of working-age Black men are out of work, and less than one out of two Black teenagers has the prospect of a job. Agriculture is in the midst of a severe depression, as slash and burn capitalism threatens to wipe out small family farms. Education cutbacks and the poverty draft are forcing millions of

"... They told me they're building it to protect our way of life ..."

people—a disproportionate number being people of color—to join the military in search of a job.

## Change Don't Come Easy

We've got a long way to go to take back this country and lift the perpetual siege. We can succeed if we realize that the key to changing foreign policy is domestic politics. There will be no new relevant spectrum for foreign policy without a new spectrum for domestic policy. So long as the country is dominated by competing elites they will define the national interest as their own, and defend it with intervention.

We can succeed if we act on the knowledge that work for peace and justice must go hand in hand, or we will never build a unified progressive movement. And without a unified progressive movement, there will be no peace and no justice. Perhaps that's been said so often it's a cliche, but that doesn't make it any less important.

We can succeed if we find ways to reach the large numbers of young people who think they'll be all they can be through Ramboism and selfish-side economics. We won't reach them with the slogan "No More Vietnams." If this generation is condemned to repeat the Vietnam War tragedy, it will be partly out of ignorance. Today's 18-year-old was born in 1968 and 5 years old when U.S. combat troops left Vietnam. At age 11, hostages were held in Iran and the country went through an orgy of anguish and hate. No thanks to Ronald Reagan, the hostages were released the day of his inauguration and, like the Olympics four years later when today's 18-year-old was 16, the celebration of American nationalism merged with the celebration of Reaganism. The stampede for Olympic gold was like the stampede over Grenada; the deck was stacked in favor of the U.S. The lesson was it's the win that counts, not how or why you get it. It's standing tall that matters, not how many backs you stand on.

We can succeed if we build international bridges rooted in a firm foundation of mutual respect and understanding. Workers in other countries are not "stealing American jobs" any more than U.S. workers are "pricing themselves out of the job market."[19] Workers everywhere have an interest in creating an economic system which rejects dependence upon cheap labor.

Popular revolutions in other countries don't threaten the United States. They threaten the same structures of oppression which exploit poor and working people here. The initiatives they undertake in literacy, cooperatives and grassroots democracy can serve as examples for Americans in the same way that progressive initiatives in the U.S. can serve as examples abroad. No people hold a monopoly on creativity and progress, and no nation should pretend to.

As residents of the reigning superpowers, U.S. and Soviet citizens have a special burden. We must not only learn to co-exist with each other, saving ourselves and the world from nuclear annihilation, we must stop our governments from ongoing intervention in the affairs of other countries. It is not the U.S. which must contain the Soviet Union and vice versa. It is the respective citizenry of each country which must see to it that other nations can control their own destinies.

The U.S. "sphere of influence" is far larger than the Soviet's, and the U.S. record of intervention is far longer. Unraveling the web which binds that sphere will be the test of our humanity, and of our own democracy-to-be.

Americans have made a difference. If not for the anti-apartheid movement, with its vital student component, Reagan's enthusiastic "constructive engagement" would still define U.S. policy toward South Africa. There would be no embargo, and no disinvestment by corporations, universities and local governments.

In Central America, intervention has not been derailed, but the pace has been slowed. If not for public pressure, the U.S. would be more deeply involved in Central America, possibly with an invasion of El Salvador and Nicaragua, certainly with more massive military aid to the contras—and, perhaps, recognition of the contras as the "legitimate" government of Nicaragua on some spit of land bombed and terrorized into submission. Without public pressure, liberals in Congress would not have achieved even limited brakes upon military intervention (e.g. the Boland Amendment). Much stronger action by the anti-intervention movement will be needed to stop the liberals from marching us two steps forward, one step back, into regional war in Central America by buying into a White House "compromise" on Nicaragua. In one insidious scenario, the Administration would pursue another negotiating charade with a perfect pretext for further escalation of the war: at the end of the stipulated period for negotiations, the Administration would blame failure to make progress upon the Sandinistas and Congress would further acquiesce to conterrevolutionary terror.

We must continue our varied efforts to change U.S. policy through education, electoral politics, grassroots organizing and civil disobedience. Thousands have taken individual and collective steps to act upon an alternate policy by breaking the economic embargo, providing aid to the Nicaraguan people and standing with Nicaraguans on the Honduran border; by boycotting the products of U.S.-backed oppressor regimes such as South Africa and Chile; by providing sanctuary to refugees from Haiti, El Salvador and Guatemala; by pledging to resist U.S. intervention in Central America and acting on that pledge in the face of so-called low-intensity warfare; by withdrawing savings from banks which invest in South Africa; by supporting the few incumbent politicians and the many more new candidates with principled opposition to intervention; and by participating in and promoting the development of concrete policy alternatives—such as the *Changing Course* program of Policy Alternatives for Central America and the Caribbean (PACCA) and the Dellums Alternative Military Budget.

We have made a difference. But a difference is not enough. As Congressman Ronald Dellums has said, "The United States can no longer control the world, but we can destroy it"[20]—piecemeal or wholesale. Now we must make a new policy.

# FOOTNOTES

**Chapter One**
1. "The Decline of U.S. Power," *Business Week*, March 12, 1979.
2. Laurence Shoup and William Minter, *Imperial Brain Trust: The Council on Foreign Relations and United States Foreign Policy* (New York: Monthly Review, 1977).
3. Orville Freemen, interviewed in the film, *Controlling Interest*, California Newsreel, San Francisco.
4. Roger Morris, *Uncertain Greatness: Henry Kissinger and Foreign Policy* (New York: Harper & Row, 1977), p. 8.
5. See Holly Sklar, *Trilateralism: The Trilateral Commission and Elite Planning for World Management* (Boston; South End Press, 1980).
6. Zbigniew Brzezinski, *Power and Principle: Memoirs of the National Security Adviser 1977-1981* (New York: Farrar, Straus and Giroux, 1983), p. 289.
7. *Boston Globe*, February 14, 1986.
8. Michael J. Crozier, Samuel P. Huntington, Joji Watanuki, *The Crisis of Democracy: Report on the Governability of Democracies to the Trilateral Commission* (New York: New York University Press, 1975), p. 93.
9. Ibid., pp. 61-62.
10. Ibid., p. 113.
11. Ibid., p. 115.
12. *Business Week*, March 12, 1979.
13. *New York Times*, October 18, 1979.
14. Brzezinski, *Power and Principle*, pp. 53-55.
15. *New York Times*, November 1, 1979.
16. Robert Armstrong and Janet Shenk, *El Salvador: The Face of Revolution* (Boston: South End Press, 1982), p. 139.
17. Ibid., pp. 149-50, 153.
18. Jimmy Carter, *Keeping Faith: Memoirs of a President* (New York: Bantam: 1982), p. 586.
19. Richard Burt; "Brzezinski on Aggression and How to Cope with It," *New York Times*, March 1980.
20. Brzezinski, *Power and Principle*, p. 49.
21. *New York Times*, January 2, 1979.
22. *Wall Street Journal*, April 30, 1980.
23. Thomas Hughes, "The Crack-Up: The Price of Collective Irresponsibility," *Foreign Policy*, Fall 1980, pp. 33, 35. Also see his article, "Carter and the Management of Contradictions," *Foreign Policy*, Summer 1978.

**Chapter Two**
1. Dimitri K. Simes, "Disciplining Soviet Power," *Foreign Policy*, Summer 1981, p. 33.
2. Thomas Hughes, "The Twilight of Internationalism," *Foreign Policy*, Winter 1985-86, p. 44.
3. *Boston Sunday Globe*, February 2, 1986.
4. *Washington Post Weekly*, March 3, 1986.
5. The Committee of Santa Fe, *A New Inter-American Policy For The Eighties* (Washington, D.C.: Council for Inter-American Security, 1980), pp. 1-2.
6. Norman Podhoretz, "The Reagan Road to Detente," *Foreign Affairs: America and the World 1984*, p. 456.
7. Michael Ferber, "Ronald Reagan's Religion as a Cause of World War III, *Coalition Close Up* (Washington, D.C.: Coalition for a New Foreign and Military Policy, Fall 1985), p. 3, citing a Reagan conversation with former California State Senator James Mills.

8. Jeane Kirkpatrick, "Dictatorships and Double Standards," *Commentary*, November 1979, p. 44.
9. "U.S. Security and Latin America," *Dictatorships and Double Standards: Rationalism and Reason in Politics* (New York: Touchstone, 1982), pp. 85-86.
10. Alexander Cockburn, "Press Clips," *Village Voice*, March 30, 1982.
11. *New York Times*, October 29, 1984.
12. Zbigniew Brzezinski, "Looking Back—and Forward," *Trialogue* No. 25, Winter 1980-81, p. 17; "What's Wrong With Reagan's Foreign Policy," *New York Times Magazine*, December 6, 1981; "A Conversation with Zbigniew Brzezinski," *Bill Moyers Journal*, WNET, New York, November 14, 1980.
13. Gerard C. Smith, Paolo Vittorelli, Kiichi Saeki, *Trilateral Security: Defense and Arms Control Policies in the 1980s*, Trilateral Commission Report No. 26 (New York: New York University Press, 1983), p. 79.
14. Ibid., p. 36.
15. David Owen, Zbigniew Brzezinski, Saburo Okita, *Democracy Must Work: A Trilateral Agenda for the Decade*, Trilateral Commission Report No. 28, (New York: New York University Press, 1984), pp. 9-11, 73.
16. See McGeorge Bundy, George F. Kennan, Robert S. McNamara, Gerard Smith, "Nuclear Weapons and the Atlantic Alliance," *Foreign Affairs*, Spring 1982.
17. The Commission on U.S.-Soviet Relations, *The Soviet Challenge: A Policy Framework for the 1980s* (New York: Council on Foreign Relations, 1981), p. 18.
18. Karl Kaiser, Winston Lord, Thierry de Montbrial, David Watt, *Western Security: What has Changed? What Should be Done?* (New York: Council on Foreign Relations, 1981), pp. 34-35.
19. Robert Tucker, "Trading Poland for the Gulf," *Harpers*, April 1981, pp. 17-18.
20. Robert Tucker, "The Purposes of American Power," *Foreign Affairs*, Winter 1980-81, p. 271.
21. Gary Hart, *A New Democracy* (New York: William Morrow and Co., 1983), p. 143.
22. Michael D. Barnes, "U.S. Policy in Central America," in Andrew J. Pierre, ed., *Third World Instability: Central America as a European-American Issue* (New York: New York University Press/Council on Foreign Relations, 1985), p. 79.
23. Alan Tonelson, "The Real National Interest," *Foreign Policy*, Winter 1985-86, p. 59.
24. Ibid., p. 51.
25. Tucker, "Purposes of American Power," p. 272.
26. Robert Tucker, "Their Wars, Our Choices," *New Republic*, October 24, 1983.
27. Tonelson, "Real National Interest," pp. 67, 71-72.
28. Robert Legvold, "Containment without Confrontation," *Foreign Policy*, Fall 1980, pp. 89, 93.
29. Report of a National Policy Panel of the United Nations Association of the USA, *U.S.-Soviet Relations: A Strategy for the '80s* (New York: UNA-USA, 1981), p. 33.
30. The Report of the Study Commission on U.S. Policy Toward Southern Africa, *South Africa: Time Running Out* (Los Angeles: University of California Press/ Foreign Policy Study Foundation, 1981), pp. xxiii-xxiv.
31. Ibid., pp. 403, 406-407, 418-19.
32. Ford Foundation mss. of Foreward to the 1986 edition, forthcoming from the University of California Press.
33. The Inter-American Dialogue, *The Americas in 1984: A Year for Decisions* (Washington, D.C.: Aspen Institute for Humanistic Studies, May 1984), pp. 29, 32, 35.
34. George Shultz, "Power and Diplomacy in the 1980s," *Trialogue* No. 36, p. 24.
35. George Shultz, "Terrorism and the Modern World," address to the Park Avenue Synagogue in Manhattan, excerpted in *New York Times*, October 26, 1984.
36. *Hearings on the Nomination of Caspar W. Weinberger to be Secretary of Defense*, Senate Committee on Armed Services, January 6, 1981, pp. 38-39.
37. *Boston Globe*, February 9, 1986.
38. *New York Times*, January 16, 1986.
39. Michael T. Klare, "Low-Intensity Conflict: The New U.S. Strategic Doctrine," *The Nation*, December 28, 1985.

40. Richard Shultz, "Low-Intensity Conflict," in Stuart M. Butler, et. al., eds., *Mandate for Leadership II: Continuing the Conservative Revolution* (Washington D.C.: Heritage Foundation, 1984), p. 264.
41. *New York Times*, June 4, 1985.

**Chapter Three**
1. Borge speech reproduced in *Sandinistas Speak* (New York: Pathfinder Press, 1982), p. 132.
2. *New York Times*, October 19, 1984, quoting Peter Teeley.
3. Mark Hertsgaard, "How Reagan Seduced Us," *Village Voice*, September 18, 1984, p. 17.
4. *New York Times*, April 30, 1985.
5. *New York Times*, July 9, 1985.
6. *New York Times*, February 28, 1986.
7. Cynthia Brown, ed., *With Friends Like These: The America's Watch Report on Human Rights and U.S. Policy in Latin America* (New York: Pantheon, 1985).
8. America's Watch, *Human Rights in Nicaragua: Reagan, Rhetoric and Reality*, July 1985.
9. Karl Bermann, *Under the Big Stick: The United States and Nicaragua Since 1848* (Boston: South End Press, forthcoming 1986), p. 395 mss.
10. Cited in Ibid.
11. Cited by Alexander Cockburn, "Beat the Devil," *The Nation*, March 31, 1984.
12. Letter in response to Jeane Kirkpatrick, *Commentary*, April 1981.
13. Walter LeFeber, *Inevitable Revolutions: The United States and Central America* (New York: W.W. Norton and Co., 1983).
14. Paul E. Sigmund, "Latin America: Change or Continuity?" *Foreign Affairs: America and the World 1981*, p. 638.
15. "Nicaragua," Latin American Forecasting Study, Business International Corporation, August 1980.
16. *New York Times*, June 11, 1984.
17. Christopher Dickey, *With the Contras: A Reporter in the Wilds of Nicaragua* (New York: Simon and Schuster, 1985) p. 146.
18. I originally developed the first three points in a report for the National Mobilization for Survival "Central America Briefing Packet, 1985," New York.
19. Robert Mathews, "The Limits of Friendship," in "Sandinista Foreign Policy," *NACLA: Report on the Americas*, May-June 1985, p. 25., citing *Congressional Presentation Document*, Security Assistance Programs, FY 1981, p. 419.
20. Ibid., p. 30.
21. NARMIC, *Invasion: A Guide to the U.S. Military Presence in Central America* (Philadelphia: American Friends Service Committee, 1985), p. 4.
22. *On a Short Fuse: Militarization in Central America*, Caribbean Basin Information Project (CBIP) Press Kit, Washington, D.C., 1985.
23. Marc Edelman, "Lifelines," in "Sandinista Foreign Policy," p. 49.
24. CBIP, *On a Short Fuse*.
25. Fred Clarkson, "Supplying the Contras," *Covert Action Information Bulletin*, Winter 1986.
26. Seymour M. Hersh, *The Price of Power: Kissinger in the Nixon White House* (New York: Summit Books, 1983), p. 265.
27. John B. Oakes, "'Fraud' in Nicaragua," *New York Times*, November 15, 1984.
28. *New York Times*, October 21, 1984.
29. Mark Cook, "The Reluctant Candidate," *The Nation*, October 13, 1984.
30. *The Electoral Process in Nicaragua: Domestic and International Influences*, Latin American Studies Association, November 19. 1984.
31. Roy Gutman, "Nicaragua: America's Diplomatic Charade," *Foreign Policy*, Fall 1984, p.4.
32. Central American Historical Institute, *Envio* 4: 54, December 1985. See also, Tom Farer, "Contadora: the Hidden Agenda," *Foreign Policy*, Summer 1985.
33. *New York Times*, August 18, 1985.
34. Barnes, "U.S. Policy in Central America," p. 85.

35. Reproduced in Reed Brody, *Contra Terror in Nicaragua* (Boston: South End Press, 1985).
36. Edgar Chamorro with Jefferson Morley, "Confessions of a 'Contra,'" *New Republic*, August 5, 1985.
37. International Court of Justice, Case Concerning Military and Paramilitary Activities in and Against Nicaragua (Nicaragua v. United States of America), Affidavit of Edgar Chamorro, September 5, 1985.
38. Arturo Cruz, "Nicaragua's Imperiled Revolution," *Foreign Affairs*, Summer 1983, p. 1044.
39. *Christian Science Monitor*, October 15, 1985.
40. Allan Nairn, "Endgame: A Special Report on U.S. Military Strategy in Central America," *NACLA: Report on the Americas*, May-June 1984.
41. See, for example, Joseph Collins with Frances Moore Lappe and Paul Rice, *Nicaragua: What Difference Could a Revolution Make?* (San Francisco: Institute for Food and Development Policy, revised edition, 1985), on developments in farming and the food system, and Valerie Miller, *Beyond Struggle and Hope: The Nicaraguan Literacy Crusade* (Westview Press, 1985).
42. Dickey, *With the Contras*, p. 257.
43. *Resource Center Bulletin*, Albuquerque, Fall 1985.

**Chapter Four**

1. Barnes, "U.S. Policy in Central America," p. 73.
2. *New York Times*, February 20, 1986.
3. Edward S. Herman and Frank Brodhead, *Demonstration Elections: U.S.-Staged Elections in the Dominican Republic, Vietnam and El Salvador* (Boston: South End Press, 1984).
4. *New York Times*, February 24, 1986; also see Kai Bird and Max Holland, "Capitol Letter," *The Nation*, March 1, 1986.
5. *New York Times*, March 8, 1986.
6. Annette Fuentes and Barbara Ehrenreich, *Women in the Global Factory* (Boston: South End Press, 1983), p. 19.
7. The Debt Crisis Network, *From Debt to Development* (Washington, D.C.: Institute for Policy Studies, 1985), p. 5.
8. Patricia Hynds, "Fighting for Freedom or Practicing Terrorism," Central American Historical Institute, Washington, D.C., August, 1985.
9. Americas Watch, *The Continuing Terror: Seventh Supplement to the Report on Human Rights in El Salvador*, September 1985.
10. Allan Nairn, "Behind the Death Squads," *The Progressive*, May 1984; also see Michael McClintock, *The American Connection: State Terror and Popular Resistance in El Salvador* (London: Zed Press, 1985).
11. Edward S. Herman, *The Real Terror Network: Terrorism in Fact and Propaganda* (Boston: South End Press, 1982), p. 8.
12. *New York Times*, January 14, 1986.
13. Gordon Adams and Jeff Colman, "The FY 1987 Defense Budget: Preliminary Analysis," Center on Budget and Policy Priorities, Washington, D.C., February 5, 1986.
14. Bill Moyers Journal, "Defense, Dissent and the Dollar," WNET/ Thirteen, May 8, 1981.
15. Ruth Leger Sivard, *World Military and Social Expenditures 1985* (Washington, D.C.. World Priorities, 1985), p. 5.
16. Ibid.
17. See Karin Stallard, Barbara Ehrenreich and Holly Sklar, *Poverty in the American Dream* (Boston: South End Press, 1983).
18. Jim Wright, "No, You Can't Have It All," *New York Times* op-ed, February 3, 1986.
19. See Gilda Haas, *Plant Closures: Myths, Realities and Responses* (Boston: South End Press, 1985).
20. Ronald V. Dellums, *Defense Sense: The Search for a Rational Military Policy* (Cambridge: Ballinger, 1983), p. 290.

# SELECTED READINGS

Albert, Michael and Dellinger, David, eds. *Beyond Survival: New Directions for the Disarmament Movement.* Boston: South End Press, 1983.

Barry, Tom, Wood, Beth and Preusch, Deb. *Dollars and Dictators.* Albuquerque: The Resource Center, 1982.

Bermann, Karl. *Under the Big Stick: The United States and Nicaragua Since 1848.* Boston: South End Press, forthcoming 1986.

Brody, Reed. *Contra Terror in Nicaragua.* Boston: South End Press, 1985.

Brown, Cynthia ed. *With Friends Like These: The Americas Watch Report on Human Rights and U.S. Policy in Latin America.* New York: Pantheon Books, 1985.

Chomsky, Noam. *Turning the Tide: U.S. Intervention in Central America and the Struggle for Peace.* Boston: South End Press. 1985.

Chomsky, Noam and Herman, Edward S. *The Political Economy of Human Rights.* Vols. I and II. Boston: South End Press, 1979.

Crawford, Alan. *Thunder on the Right: The 'New Right' and the Politics of Resentment.* New York: Pantheon, 1980.

Danaher, Kevin. *In Whose Interests? A Guide to U.S.-South Africa Relations.* Washington, D.C.: Institute for Policy Studies, 1984.

Dellums, Ronald V. *Defense Sense: The Search for a Rational Military Policy.* Cambridge, MA: Ballinger, 1983.

Dickey, Christopher. *With the Contras: A Reporter in the Wilds of Nicaragua.* New York: Simon & Schuster, 1985.

Dugger, Ronnie. *On Reagan: The Man and His Presidency.* New York: McGraw-Hill, 1983.

Fuentes, Annette and Ehrenreich, Barbara. *Women in the Global Factory.* Boston: South End Press, 1983.

Gettleman, Marvin E. et. al. *El Salvador: Central America in the New Cold War.* New York: Grove Press, 1981.

Herman, Edward S. *The Real Terror Network: Terrorism in Fact and Propaganda.* Boston: South End Press, 1982.

Herman, Edward S. and Brodhead, Frank. *Demonstration Elections: U.S. Staged Elections in the Dominican Republic, Vietnam and El Salvador.* Boston: South End Press, 1984.

Hersh, Seymour M. *The Price of Power: Kissinger in the Nixon White House.* New York: Summit Books, 1983.

Hofstadter, Richard. *The Paranoid Style in American Politics and Other Essays.* Chicago: The University of Chicago Press, 1979.

Klare, Michael T. *American Arms Supermarket.* Austin: University of Texas Press, 1984.

PACCA (Policy Alternatives for the Caribbean and Central America). *Changing Course: Blueprint for Peace in Central America and the Caribbean.* Washington, D.C.: Institute for Policy Studies, 1984.

Rosset, Peter and Vandermeer, John. *The Nicaragua Reader.* New York: Grove Press. 1983.

Rothenberg, Randall. *The Neo-Liberals.* New York: Simon & Schuster, 1984.

Sanders, Jerry W. *Peddlers of Crisis: The Committee on the Present Danger and the Politics of Containment.* Boston: South End Press, 1983.

Sklar, Holly, ed. *Trilateralism: The Trilateral Commission and Elite Planning for World Management.* Boston: South End Press, 1980.

Shoup, Laurence H. and Minter, William. *Imperial Brain Trust: The Council on Foreign Relations and United States Foreign Policy.* New York: Monthly Review Press, 1977.

Steinfels, Peter. *The Neoconservatives.* New York: Simon & Schuster, 1979.

# RESOURCE ORGANIZATIONS

Africa News
PO Box 3851
Durham, NC 27702

American Committee on Africa
198 Broadway
New York, NY 10038

American Friends Service Committee
1501 Cherry Street
Philadelphia, PA 19102

Center for Constitutional Rights
853 Broadway
New York, NY 10003

Center for Defense Information
303 Capitol Gallery West
600 Maryland Ave. SW
Washington, DC 20024

Center for Third World Organizing
3861 Martin Luther King Jr. Way
Oakland, CA 94609

Central American Historical Institute
*Update, Envio*
Intercultural Center, Georgetown U.
Washington, DC 20057

Central America Resource Center
PO Box 2327
Austin, TX 78768

CISPES (Committee in Solidarity
with the People of El Salvador)
Box 50139
Washington, DC 20004

Clergy and Laity Concerned
198 Broadway
New York, NY 10038

Coalition for a New Foreign and
Military Policy
712 G Street SE
Washington, DC 20003

*Covert Action Information Bulletin*
PO Box 50272
Washington, DC 20004

Data Center
464 19th Street
Oakland, CA 94612

Defense Budget Project
Center on Budget and Policy Priorities
236 Massachusetts Ave NE
Washington, DC 20002

Institute for Defense and Disarmament
Studies
251 Harvard Street
Brookline, MA 02146

Institute for Food and Development Policy
2588 Mission Street
San Francisco, CA 94110

Institute for Policy Studies
1901 Q Street NW
Washington, DC 20009

Interfaith Action for Economic Justice
110 Maryland Ave. NE
Washington, DC 20009

Interfaith Center on Corporate Responsibility
475 Riverside Dr., Room 556
New York, NY 10115

Jobs with Peace Campaign
76 Summer Street
Boston, MA 02110

Middle East Research & Information Project
*MERIP REPORTS*
P.O. Box 3122
Washington, DC 20010

NARMIC (National Action/Research
on the Military Industrial Complex)
1501 Cherry Street
Philadelphia, PA 19102

National Labor Committee in Support of
Democracy and Human Rights in El Salvador
15 Union Square
New York, NY 10003

National Mobilization for Survival
853 Broadway
New York, NY 10003

National Network in Solidarity
with the Nicaraguan People (NNSNP)
2025 I Street NW
Washington, DC 20006

NISGUA (National Network in Solidarity with
the People of Guatemala)
930 F Street NW
Washington, DC 20004

North American Congress on Latin America
*NACLA Report on the Americas*
151 W. 19th Street
New York, NY 10011